So you really want to learn

Science Prep
Book 1

Independent Schools
Examinations Board

GALORE PARK

So you really want to learn

Science Prep
Book 1

By W. R Pickering B.Sc., Ph.D., M.I.Biol., C.Biol., F.L.S.

Edited by Louise Martine B.Sc. (Lon)

Independent Schools
Examinations Board

GALORE PARK

Published by ISEB Publications, an imprint of
Galore Park Publishing Ltd,
P.O. Box 96, Cranbrook, Kent TN17 4WS
www.galorepark.co.uk

Typography and layout by Typetechnique, London W1
Printed and bound by Ashford Colour Press, Hants
Cover design by GKA Design, London WC2H

ISBN 1 902984 21 8

First published 2003

Also available:
Teacher's book   ISBN 1 902984 22 6

Acknowledgements

I should like to acknowledge the help given to me in the generation of the two characters, Material Girl and Professor Particle, by two of my students, India Cash and Zara Fitton. I should also like to acknowledge the continued support of Form 9-3 at the Altrincham Girls Grammar School with their regular supplies of chocolate at moments of crisis.

I would like to dedicate this volume to my wife Janet, my sons Chris and Tom, and my long-term furry companions Moth and Topsy.

W. R. Pickering
May 2003

The publishers would like to thank Peter Hodgson and Sue Hunter for their invaluable comments during the production of this book.

The 3-D cartoons used in this book are © www.animationfactory.com.

The drawings were supplied by Graham Edwards.

This publication includes images from CorelDRAW ® 9 which are protected by the copyright laws of the U.S., Canada and elsewhere. Used under license.

Photographs were supplied by the Science Photo Library: **p.4, 79**t, **81** Andrew Syred; **p13**t Andrew Harmer; **p13**b Dr Jeremy Burgess; **p79**m Mike Miller; **p79**b, **p119** Astrid & Hanns-Frieder Michler; **p149** John Mead; **p150** Martin Bond; **p154** John Heseltine; **p203** E.R. Degginger. All other photographs are © W.R. Pickering.

b = bottom, m = middle, t = top.

Introduction

To study science is one of the most exciting adventures you can possibly imagine. Scientists study the whole world from the huge galaxies to the tiniest microbe and, even smaller, down to molecules, atoms, nuclei and the ultimate building blocks of matter. They trace the evolution of the universe from the Big Bang to the present time. They have found out how the nuclei of atoms were made inside stars, and can describe how the universe gradually evolved to produce all the plants, fishes and animals we see today. It is a wonderful world, made by God especially for us.

Just look around you with the curiosity that leads to science. How can birds fly, why are there bright colours on a patch of oily water, why does water make a noise when it boils? Why is grass green and the sky blue? What is lightning and thunder, and where do rainbows come from? Why are crystals and snowflakes and cacti so beautifully symmetrical? Such simple questions are golden threads that can lead you to the deepest mysteries of the universe.

To find out about all this, you have to begin by learning how scientists classify plants and animals, and measure the properties of things. You will soon begin to understand the different forms of energy, how light travels and how electricity lights our homes and drives our trains.

This is just the book to start you on the great adventure called science. It will open your eyes to our wonderful world, stimulate your imagination and guide your first steps along the road of science.

Dr. Peter Hodgson, Fellow of Corpus Christi College, Oxford

About the author

Ron Pickering has published a number of very successful books covering the GCSE and A Level syllabus and has worked in both maintained and independent education for more than 20 years.

Contents

Life and living processes

Materials and their properties

Physical processes

Introduction: What is science?

Science is our organised knowledge of the natural world. You will see as we go through the book how scientists are always trying to find ways of putting everything around us into groups. This process helps us to understand why certain types of things behave or work in the way they do. We spend our lives discovering and finding out things and so not surprisingly science is a subject that affects every one of us. Watching television, taking a bus, listening to CDs, playing on a Gameboy, getting treatment from a doctor, all these (and many more) are ways that Science has an impact on our lives. Studying Science is very important because it helps us to **understand** the world around us. It is very useful, and very interesting, to know exactly why you should wash your hands after going to the loo. In the same way you might want to know why you can see yourself in a mirror, why members of conservation organisations tell us we should protect endangered species and why we should be concerned about how we are going to get our energy in the future. Studying Science can help to provide some of the answers to these questions.

There are many amazing discoveries being made in the world today. New facts, about how and why things happen the way they do, are discovered by scientists all the time.

About this book

As we go through this book we will begin our study of Science and we will start to find things out for ourselves. How many times in your life have you asked questions such as "why does it do that?" or "why doesn't it do that?" Asking these sorts of questions is the first step to becoming a scientist. Hopefully you will enjoy learning about your world and find our three scientists entertaining as they show you around.

The way scientists start to find things out is by carrying out **experiments**. For example, a scientist might want to find out why petrol burns to produce heat. It is really important that experiments are carried out following certain rules, so that their results will be reliable. Scientists need to be sure that their results are reliable before they can say they have really found something out.

There are loads of different kinds of scientist, and here are just some that you may have come across:

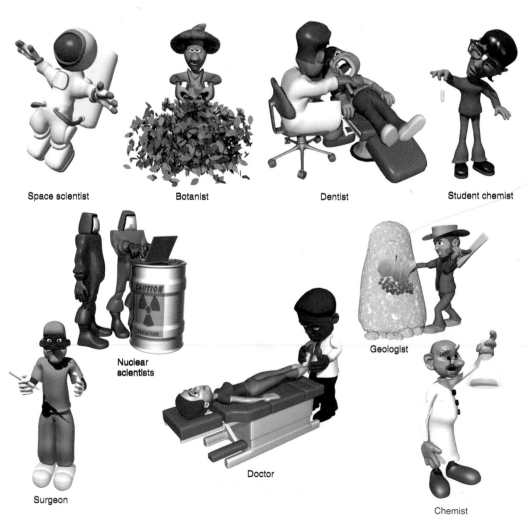

Space scientist

Botanist

Dentist

Student chemist

Nuclear scientists

Geologist

Doctor

Surgeon

Chemist

Whatever they do, scientists need to be very careful with their experiments. Don't forget experiments aren't just about blowing things up in a chemistry lab; they could be as safe as watching how a bee flies from flower to flower collecting pollen, and how it then takes the pollen away and makes honey. In this book we will see some of the things we have found out from the results of experiments carried out by scientists. We will also be told about the rules we need to stick to, so that we too can carry out experiments in a reliable way.

There are three parts to this book:

- **Living processes:** This is where we learn about the lives of animals and plants and that includes you! Bioman is the chap who will take you on a guided tour and help you understand these living processes. He also has some very interesting things which he will tell you, so look out for those red boxes!

- **Materials and their properties:** In this part we deal with the different chemicals in our world. You will see how different materials have useful properties, as well as how some of these materials can be changed from one form to another. This time you will be helped by Minnie the Material Girl who can be found whizzing around on her skateboard or scooter!

- **Physical processes:** Professor Particle will help explain some of the things that happen in the world around you. You will find out about electricity, forces, light and sound. You will also get an idea of what scientists know about the Universe beyond the Earth.

Bioman   Material Girl   Professor Particle

Chapter 1
Life processes

We will begin by looking at the living world around us. The things in the pictures below may look very *different* from each other, but there is one way in which they are all the *same:* they are all **alive**. We know that they are alive because they show the **characteristics of life**. All living organisms can carry out certain processes which give them these characteristics of life. There are seven **life processes,** four of which are shown in the diagram on the right. Start thinking about what the missing three might be because there is a question about them at the end of the section.

A mammal

A plant

Fungi

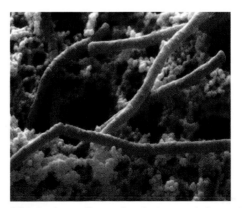

Microbe (a small organism that can only be seen with a microscope)

Life processes in animals

Life processes in plants

MOVEMENT: Animals can change their position. They can move their whole body when they go from one place to another. They can also move parts of their body – for example when a human lifts an arm to put food into the mouth.

REPRODUCTION: Animals can produce offspring. These offspring (baby animals) eventually grow into adults like their parents.

GROWTH: Small animals get bigger and eventually become adults. They can't do this unless nutrition provides all of the raw materials and energy needed.

NUTRITION: Eating food provides an animal with the materials it needs to build up its body and to give it energy.

REPRODUCTION: Plants can produce offspring. These often grow from seeds and eventually grow into adult plants like their parents.

GROWTH: Small plants get bigger and eventually become adults. They can't do this unless nutrition provides all of the raw materials and energy needed.

NUTRITION: Food provides a plant with the materials it needs to build up its body and to give it energy.

Although all living organisms carry out these life processes, they may not carry out them out in the same way. A cat can move very quickly when it chases a mouse, but flower petals only move very slowly when a flower opens up in the morning. When you, a human, put food into your mouth, that is when the feeding process starts, whereas a plant only begins to feed itself when it is able to trap sunlight and absorb water and nutrients through its roots. We'll see how a plant does this in the plant section of this book.

Scientists try to find out more about life and living things by studying how animals and plants carry out these life processes. The branch of science concerned with the study of living things is called **Biology.** This comes from the ancient Greek word "bios" meaning "life".

Dead or alive?

All living things, called organisms, are made up of tiny structures called **cells**. A human body is made from billions of cells. Most of these cells are far too small to see with the naked eye, but some scientists many years ago developed a piece of kit called a **microscope** which allows us to see some of these cells.

Dead things used to be alive, so they are still made of cells, but because they are dead they can no longer carry out the life processes.

Things that have never lived (sometimes called **non-living** things) are not made from cells. They have never carried out any life processes and never could.

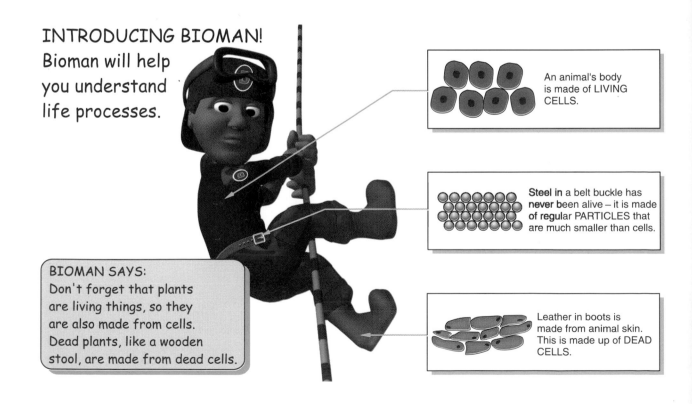

INTRODUCING BIOMAN!
Bioman will help you understand life processes.

An animal's body is made of LIVING CELLS.

Steel in a belt buckle has **never** been alive – it is made of regular PARTICLES that are much smaller than cells.

BIOMAN SAYS:
Don't forget that plants are living things, so they are also made from cells. Dead plants, like a wooden stool, are made from dead cells.

Leather in boots is made from animal skin. This is made up of DEAD CELLS.

Exercise 1.1: Life processes

1. (a) Write down the life processes common to plants and give a short description of each.

   (b) There are seven life processes common to animals, four of which are described in the diagram on page 5. By using books or the internet, find out what the 'missing' three are and write a short description of each.

2. Look at this list. Say whether each thing is living, **dead** or **non-living**.

   A CAT CHASING ITS TAIL

   A WOODEN CHAIR

   A STAINLESS STEEL SPOON

   A LEATHER COAT

   A DRINKING GLASS

   A ROTTING TOMATO

   A COTTON T-SHIRT

Extension questions

3. Movement in most animals can be easily seen. Movement in plants is far less obvious. Write a sentence to describe what movement you might see in a daisy.

4. Design an experiment to discover whether a plant moves towards the light as it grows.

Made for the job

Each part of the body of a living organism has a different job to do. The body is constructed in such a way that it can carry out all of the life processes it needs to perform in order to stay alive. When you look at the different parts of an animal or a plant, you should try to see how each part is suited to the job it has to do.

These two diagrams show how the bodies of plants and animals are 'made for the job'.

Plants and life processes

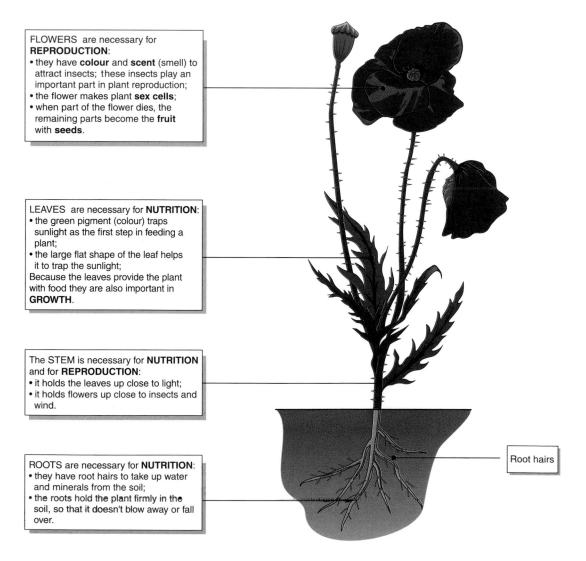

FLOWERS are necessary for **REPRODUCTION**:
• they have **colour** and **scent** (smell) to attract insects; these insects play an important part in plant reproduction;
• the flower makes plant **sex cells**;
• when part of the flower dies, the remaining parts become the **fruit** with **seeds**.

LEAVES are necessary for **NUTRITION**:
• the green pigment (colour) traps sunlight as the first step in feeding a plant;
• the large flat shape of the leaf helps it to trap the sunlight;
Because the leaves provide the plant with food they are also important in **GROWTH**.

The STEM is necessary for **NUTRITION** and for **REPRODUCTION**:
• it holds the leaves up close to light;
• it holds flowers up close to insects and wind.

ROOTS are necessary for **NUTRITION**:
• they have root hairs to take up water and minerals from the soil;
• the roots hold the plant firmly in the soil, so that it **doesn't** blow away or fall over.

Root hairs

Animals and life processes

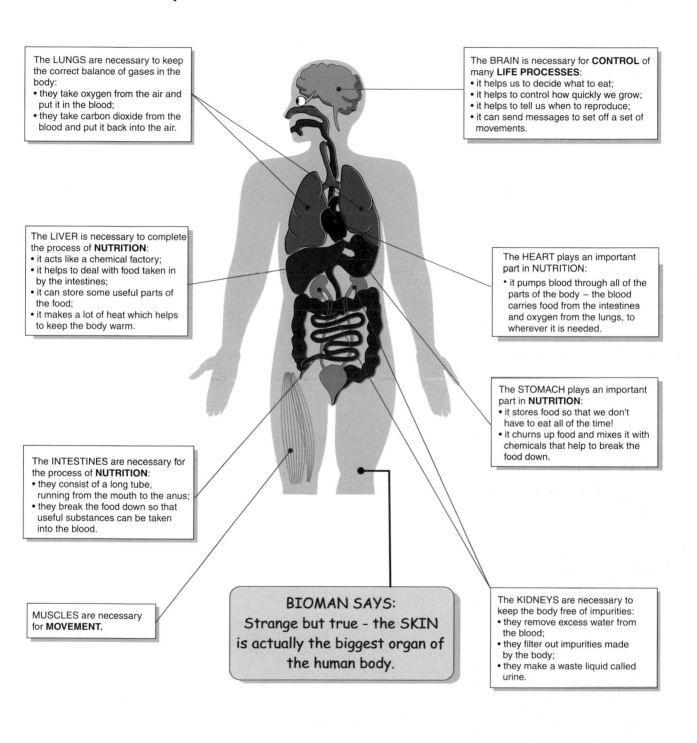

The LUNGS are necessary to keep the correct balance of gases in the body:
- they take oxygen from the air and put it in the blood;
- they take carbon dioxide from the blood and put it back into the air.

The BRAIN is necessary for **CONTROL** of many **LIFE PROCESSES**:
- it helps us to decide what to eat;
- it helps to control how quickly we grow;
- it helps to tell us when to reproduce;
- it can send messages to set off a set of movements.

The LIVER is necessary to complete the process of **NUTRITION**:
- it acts like a chemical factory;
- it helps to deal with food taken in by the intestines;
- it can store some useful parts of the food;
- it makes a lot of heat which helps to keep the body warm.

The HEART plays an important part in NUTRITION:
- it pumps blood through all of the parts of the body – the blood carries food from the intestines and oxygen from the lungs, to wherever it is needed.

The STOMACH plays an important part in **NUTRITION**:
- it stores food so that we don't have to eat all of the time!
- it churns up food and mixes it with chemicals that help to break the food down.

The INTESTINES are necessary for the process of **NUTRITION**:
- they consist of a long tube, running from the mouth to the anus;
- they break the food down so that useful substances can be taken into the blood.

MUSCLES are necessary for **MOVEMENT.**

BIOMAN SAYS:
Strange but true - the SKIN is actually the biggest organ of the human body.

The KIDNEYS are necessary to keep the body free of impurities:
- they remove excess water from the blood;
- they filter out impurities made by the body;
- they make a waste liquid called urine.

Exercise 1.2: 'Made for the job'

1. (a) Match up the words in the first column with the descriptions in the second column.

    Stomach   Pumps blood around an animal's body

    Heart   Remove impurities from the blood

    Lungs   Controls many of the life processes in animals

    Kidneys   Allow oxygen to enter the body

    Brain   Stores and churns food

    Liver   Deals with food taken into the body through the intestines

    (b) Draw a simple outline of a human body. Mark on it where you would find the brain, heart, lungs, stomach, intestines, liver and kidneys.

2. (a) Match up the words in the first column with the descriptions in the second column.

    Leaf   Make the plant's sex cells

    Roots   Holds leaves up close to the light

    Stem   Absorb minerals from the soil

    Flowers   Traps sunlight

    (b) Examine a real flowering plant specimen (or the picture on page 8 if you don't have one). Draw a simple diagram and label the roots, stem, leaves and flower.

3. Name the two important substances an animal must take in to survive.

Extension question

4. Think about how plants and animals differ in the way they feed themselves. Explain how this difference means that plants don't need to move much but animals do.

Adaptation and survival

Don't forget

So far we have learnt that:

- Living organisms need to carry out certain life processes in order to live.
- Nutrition (feeding) provides the building blocks and energy to carry out the other life processes.

Living organisms must be able to feed themselves if they are going to be able to carry out their life processes. They obtain their food from their environment, and often have special features to help them do this. As we know, on our planet there are many different types of environments, from the very hot to the very cold and from the dry to the wet. We can find living organisms in all these different places because they have developed "special features" that enable them to cope with their own particular environment.

A feature that helps an organism to survive in its environment is called an **adaptation**. Understanding adaptation is a very important part of the study of Biology. Some examples are shown in these photographs.

A LION needs to get its food by catching and eating other animals. It lives in the grasslands of Africa, and shows several adaptations:

- *It has piercing teeth (canines) and cutting teeth to deal with a diet of meat.*
- *It is coloured, so that it is well-camouflaged and able to creep up close to its prey and pounce on the unsuspecting victim!*
- *It has powerful muscles that enable it to leap onto its prey and pull it to the ground.*

An OSPREY lives on fish which it captures by diving down and pulling them from the water.
- *It has powerful talons (claws) to hold on to slippery fish.*
- *It has a hooked beak to tear the flesh from the fish.*
- *It has long, broad wings, so that it can fly and carry its prey at the same time.*

A FROG is an amphibian, and spends some of its time on land and some in water.
- *It has webbed feet and long hind legs which are very powerful and help it to swim away from its predators.*
- *It has eyes and nostrils on the top of its head and can remain mostly hidden under water whilst still breathing and watching for food.*
- *It has a sticky tongue for catching prey such as dragonflies.*
- *When the breeding season comes, the male gets sticky pads on his hands to hold onto the slippery female during mating.*

A STICKLEBACK is a fish, and lives in ponds and streams in the UK.
- It has gills to allow it to take oxygen from the water.
- It has a streamlined shape to help it to swim efficiently through the water.
- It has fins to push against the water and make movement easier.

A WOODPECKER is a bird that lives in woodlands and feeds on the grubs of insects.
- It has a pointed beak, like a spike which it uses to drill into trees to find its food. You can often hear its rapid tapping sound if you listen hard enough in wooded areas.
- It has a long tongue with a sharp tip that reaches into the tunnels in the tree trunk where the grubs are hiding.
- It has a short, stiff tail so that it can prop itself up on the tree whilst it drills for grubs.

A DESERT CACTUS lives in a very dry environment but still needs to trap sunlight to make its food.
- The leaves have changed into spines which helps to protect the cactus against animals that might want to eat it. You wouldn't want a mouth full of prickly spines!
- It has a thick swollen stem that is very good for storing water.
- It has very long roots that reach down far into the soil to collect whatever water there is.

A SUNDEW is a plant that lives in damp, boggy places where many of the minerals in the soil have been washed away.
- It has extra leaves which are very sticky. These can trap insects, so that the sundew plant can get its minerals from the insects' bodies; it literally "eats" them!
- It has normal leaves which are well spread out to trap the maximum amount of sunlight.

Exercise 1.3: Adaptation and survival

1. Write down one special adaptation which would be needed to enable:

   (a) the leaves of a plant to avoid being eaten by deer;

   (b) a small mammal to feed on nuts that only grow at the top of a tree;

   (c) a fish to live on the bottom of the sea;

   (d) a snail to live on a rocky shore where it can be pounded by waves;

   (e) a lizard to avoid being eaten by birds in a sandy desert;

   (f) a flower to attract an insect that does not have a sense of smell.

2. The diagram shows a swallow. This bird feeds on insects that it catches while it is flying. It needs to migrate to Africa during our winter because there aren't enough insects here to feed it. Explain two ways in which it is adapted to survive in its environment.

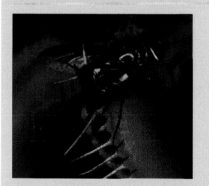

3. The photograph shows a plant called a Venus fly trap. Find out how it feeds itself and how it is adapted to do this.

Chapter 2
Nutrition in animals: using teeth

Let's start our discovery of living organisms by looking at the animal kingdom and that of course includes you! We will deal with plants later on in the book.

Don't forget

- Animals must feed to carry out their life processes.
- In order to survive different environments, living organisms have adapted their features.

Animals get their food from the environment. The first step of the process is actually to get the food into the mouth. Once the food is in the mouth it needs to be cut up and mixed with saliva to make it easier to swallow. The **teeth** play a very important part in this. The food can come in all shapes and sizes, so it shouldn't be a surprise to find that there are several different types of teeth.

Humans have four different types of teeth. Each is adapted to a different job and not surprisingly is quite different in shape. These are shown in the diagram below:

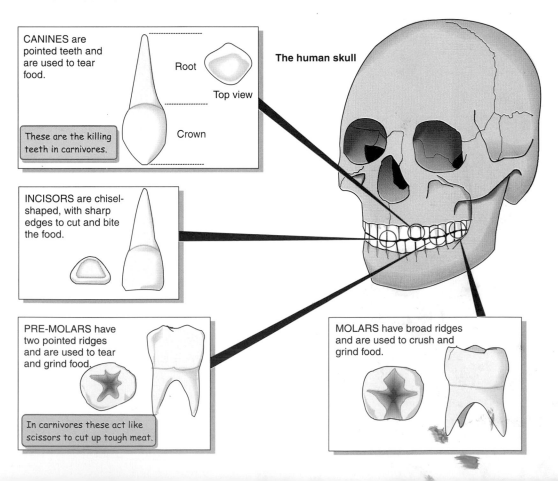

CANINES are pointed teeth and are used to tear food.

These are the killing teeth in carnivores.

Root

Top view

Crown

The human skull

INCISORS are chisel-shaped, with sharp edges to cut and bite the food.

PRE-MOLARS have two pointed ridges and are used to tear and grind food.

In carnivores these act like scissors to cut up tough meat.

MOLARS have broad ridges and are used to crush and grind food.

When do we get our teeth?

You have two sets of teeth during your lifetime. The teeth grow out of holes called **sockets** in the jawbone. A baby starts to get its first set of teeth (called the **milk teeth**) when it is about six months old, and it may take up to three years for the complete set of twenty teeth to appear. The milk teeth start to be replaced by the **permanent teeth** from about six years old. As the new permanent teeth grow they start to push the milk teeth out. That's when your first teeth become wobbly and fall out and if you're lucky enough the tooth fairy pays a visit and leaves behind some cash! By the time humans are 12-13 years old all the milk teeth should have gone and have been replaced by 28 of the permanent teeth: eight incisors, four canines, eight premolars and eight molars.

If the jaw is long enough, four more molars may appear in the late teens or early twenties. Because these teeth appear when you are more mature they are sometimes called **wisdom teeth**.

Caring for the teeth

If the teeth are not looked after, they can decay and eventually fall out. Decayed teeth look horrid and can make your breath smell very bad. They also don't chew up food very well. Decay is caused by bacteria which change the sugar left on your teeth, after you have eaten something sweet, into acid. The acid then eats away the hard enamel covering on the teeth, making a hole which finally reaches the soft insides. That's when you get toothache because the soft inside of the teeth is very, very sensitive. This decaying process is shown in the diagram below:

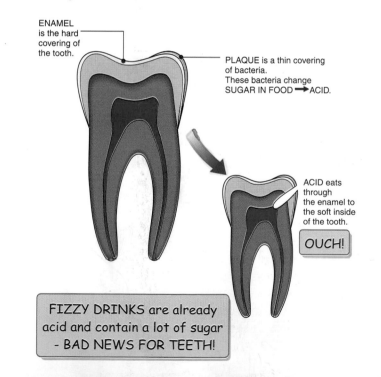

ENAMEL is the hard covering of the tooth.

PLAQUE is a thin covering of bacteria. These bacteria change SUGAR IN FOOD ➡ ACID.

ACID eats through the enamel to the soft inside of the tooth.

OUCH!

FIZZY DRINKS are already acid and contain a lot of sugar - BAD NEWS FOR TEETH!

We can prevent tooth decay and all those painful visits to the dentist by trying to follow these simple rules:

● avoid sugar in the food you eat;

● prevent the build up of bacteria on your teeth.

It is almost impossible not to get sugar in your diet, but it is easier to prevent the build up of bacteria (**plaque**) by cleaning your teeth properly. This is how you should brush you teeth:

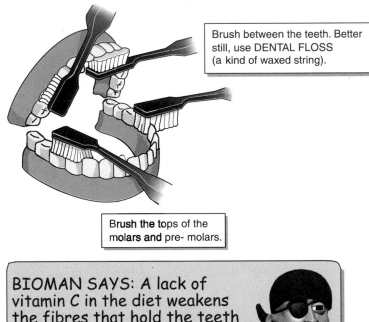

Brush both the back and the front of the teeth. Always brush away from the gum or the gum may be damaged.

Brush between the teeth. Better still, use DENTAL FLOSS (a kind of waxed string).

Brush the tops of the molars and pre- molars.

BIOMAN SAYS: A lack of vitamin C in the diet weakens the fibres that hold the teeth to the jaw. Old-time sailors on long voyages without fresh food often had the disease scurvy. This caused their teeth to fall out and their gums to bleed.

Fluoride and your teeth

There's something else that helps resist tooth decay and that's a mineral called fluoride. Fluoride is found in water. It strengthens the tooth enamel and helps to combat tooth decay by making it harder for the acid to eat into the enamel. In some parts of the country, naturally-occurring fluoride levels are low, so the Local Authorities add it to the drinking water. Dentists can also put it directly onto the teeth using a special jelly.

Exercise 2.1: Teeth

1. Name four things that you would teach a child as it is growing up, so that it had good, strong teeth as an adult.

2. (a) Match up the names of teeth (list 1) with the descriptions of what they do (list 2).

   List 1: Incisors, canines, premolars, molars.

   List 2: Tearing and grinding of food; tearing of food, and killing in some cases; cutting and biting of food; crushing and grinding of food.

   (b) Draw a simple diagram of each of the four main kinds of teeth. Label the features of the teeth that make them able to perform the jobs they do.

Extension question

3. The diagrams below show plans of the teeth in the upper and lower jaw. Plan A is from a 27-year-old man called James, plan B is from a 27-year-old man called David.

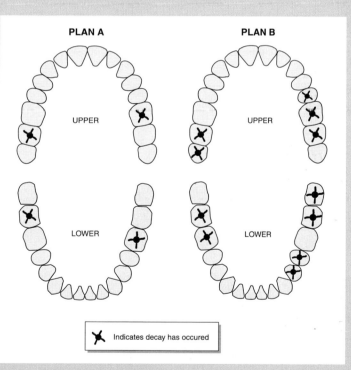

The two men live in different towns. In one town the natural drinking water contains fluoride salts, but there are no fluoride salts in the drinking water of the other town.

(a) Which man do you think lives in the town with fluoride in the drinking water? Explain your answer.

(b) Suggest other reasons for the difference in the number of decayed teeth between the two men.

(c) Most of the decayed teeth are cheek teeth, i.e. the molars. Suggest a reason for this.

Nutrition: a balanced diet

Now we know how important teeth are, we can think about the food they chew up. Food is vital to all living organisms; without food, the essential life processes cease and you die.

We need food:

- to supply the substances which will become the **raw materials** for growth and for mending damaged parts of the body;
- to provide a **source of energy**, so that these raw materials can be built into cells and body parts;
- to supply elements and compounds that make sure the raw materials and energy are used efficiently.

All living organisms have these requirements. Some organisms, the green plants for example, can make their own food substances (see page 35). Other organisms *cannot* make their own food, and must take in foods from their surroundings. Humans, like all other animals, are totally dependent on other organisms for their supply of food substances.

The total of all of these food substances or **nutrients** is called the **diet**. A healthy diet provides a human with the *balanced* selection of nutrients which it needs to carry out its life processes. If the diet does not provide all of the nutrients in the correct proportions the person may suffer from **malnutrition.** Have a look at the diagram below and think about where you would be on the scale!

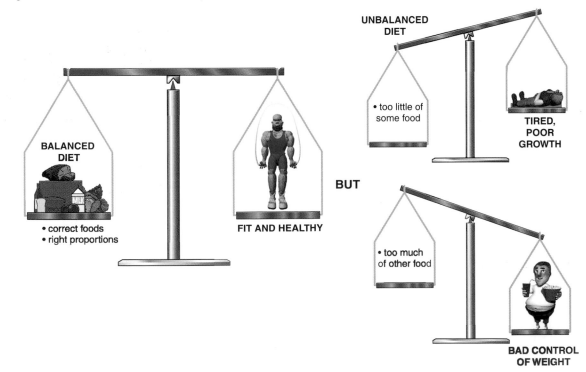

BALANCED DIET
- correct foods
- right proportions

FIT AND HEALTHY

BUT

UNBALANCED DIET
- too little of some food

TIRED, POOR GROWTH

- too much of other food

BAD CONTROL OF WEIGHT

A balanced diet should contain:

- carbohydrates, such as sugars and starches
- proteins
- fats
- mineral salts
- vitamins
- water
- fibre

Bioman certainly looks as though he eats a balanced diet!

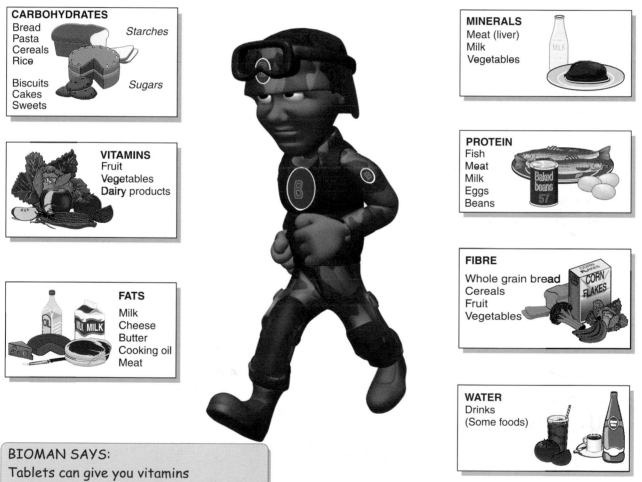

CARBOHYDRATES
Bread
Pasta
Cereals
Rice

Starches

Biscuits
Cakes
Sweets

Sugars

VITAMINS
Fruit
Vegetables
Dairy products

FATS
Milk
Cheese
Butter
Cooking oil
Meat

MINERALS
Meat (liver)
Milk
Vegetables

PROTEIN
Fish
Meat
Milk
Eggs
Beans

FIBRE
Whole grain bread
Cereals
Fruit
Vegetables

WATER
Drinks
(Some foods)

BIOMAN SAYS:
Tablets can give you vitamins
and minerals, but a balanced diet is best!

Carbohydrates which include starches and sugars, supply most of the **energy** we need. Starches are usually better than sugars because:

- the body breaks them down more slowly, so we feel fuller for longer;
- they don't cause such problems of tooth decay.

Proteins are used for the **growth and repair** of cells.

Fats provide a supply of **energy**. We can store lots of fat beneath our skin, where it can act as padding and help to keep us warm.

Minerals are substances that usually combine with another food to form different parts of the body, such as teeth, bones and red blood cells. We usually get minerals from food such as meat.

Vitamins are substances that are needed in very small amounts to enable the body to use the other nutrients more efficiently. There are many of them, and they are usually taken in with other foods, especially dairy products. You can also take vitamin tablets which are particularly good if your diet is not a very balanced one!

Water forms about 70% of the human body which is a pretty amazing fact! Two-thirds of this water is in the cells, and the other third is in the blood.

Humans lose about 1.5 litres of water each day in urine, faeces, exhaled air and sweat and so it must be replaced by water in the diet. We replace this water in two main ways:

i. as a drink; and

ii. in food, especially in salad foods like tomato and lettuce.

Dietary fibre is the indigestible component of the food (largely from plant cell walls) which provides bulk for the faeces. As a result the muscles of the intestines are stretched and can push the food along. A shortage of fibre can cause constipation, and may be a factor in the development of bowel cancer.

> **BIOMAN'S SUMMARY:**
> A balanced diet contains fats, proteins, carbohydrates, vitamins, minerals, water and fibre in the correct proportions to supply enough energy and raw materials for the processes of life.

Exercise 2.2: A balanced diet

1. Copy and complete the following passage:

   Food is needed for all living organisms. It provides a source of .... .To remain fit and healthy you need to eat a balanced .... A balanced diet should contain ...., ..., ..., ..., ..., ..., and water.

2. Match up the words in the first list with the functions in the second list. Choose the best match in each case.

   LIST 1: fish, butter, spaghetti, milk, wholemeal bread, lettuce.
   LIST 2: can provide a lot of our water needs; a good food for body-builders; a main source of energy; dairy product that can supply energy and some vitamins; helps prevent constipation; excellent source of vitamins and minerals – an ideal baby food!

3. Look at the food labels on a packet of crisps, a yoghurt and a packet of breakfast cereal. How many grams of fat are there in a 100 g portion of each? Which food provides the most fat, and which the least?

Chapter 3
Moving materials around the body: blood and the heart

Once the food has been swallowed and digested, the products need to be transported to all parts of the body, from the top of your head to the tips of your toes!

Starting points

- By now you know living organisms need food in order to survive, and in animals this food is taken into the body through the intestines.
- Once the food is absorbed by the intestines, it needs to be carried to all parts of the body and this is where the blood and heart come in!

The cells that make up the bodies of all living organisms need a supply of food. They also need a supply of oxygen, so that they can extract energy from the food. Looking back to page 9 we can see that food is absorbed from the intestines and oxygen is obtained from the lungs. This food and oxygen are taken to all the cells in the body by the circulatory system. The **circulatory system** which is shown below, is made up of three parts:

- the blood, a red fluid that can dissolve oxygen and foods;
- the heart, that acts like a pump to push the blood around the body; and
- the blood vessels, the arteries, capillaries and veins, that make sure that the blood circulates to the places it's needed.

ARTERIES carry blood away from the heart and to the cells of the body.

OXYGEN from lungs

HEART is the pump for the circulation.

VEINS carry blood away from the cells and back to the heart.

FOOD from intestines

CAPILLARIES allow food and gases to pass between the blood and the cells.

BIOMAN SAYS: Earthworms have 5 hearts! You can see a big blood vessel on the top side of an earthworm's body.

The heart: the pump for the circulation

The heart pumps the blood around the body. It does this by putting pressure on the blood and squeezing it into the blood vessels. The heart can do this because it is really one big mass of very powerful muscle. The structure of the heart is shown in the diagram below; you can see that it is made up of four chambers. Two of the chambers receive blood, and two of them pump it out again.

Your heart beats often enough to keep delivering a good supply of food and oxygen to the cells that need these substances, even when you are asleep. Every beat of the heart makes the walls of the arteries stretch slightly. This 'stretching' can be felt anywhere that an artery passes over a bone near to the skin. This stretching movement is called a **pulse**.

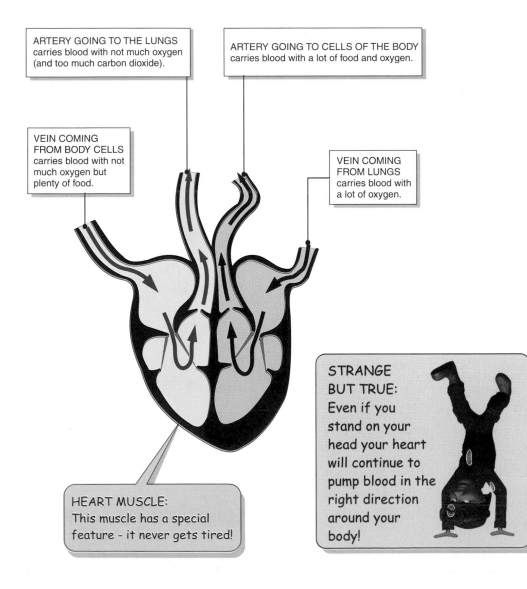

ARTERY GOING TO THE LUNGS
carries blood with not much oxygen (and too much carbon dioxide).

ARTERY GOING TO CELLS OF THE BODY
carries blood with a lot of food and oxygen.

VEIN COMING FROM BODY CELLS
carries blood with not much oxygen but plenty of food.

VEIN COMING FROM LUNGS
carries blood with a lot of oxygen.

HEART MUSCLE:
This muscle has a special feature - it never gets tired!

STRANGE BUT TRUE:
Even if you stand on your head your heart will continue to pump blood in the right direction around your body!

Where does the oxygen come from?
The lungs and breathing

The lungs are the parts of the body that enable oxygen to enter the blood. They are found in the chest, very close to the heart and this seems extremely sensible since the heart has to pump blood to the lungs in order to collect oxygen. Every time we breathe in we supply fresh air to the lungs, so that more oxygen can pass into the blood, and every time we breathe out we get rid of a waste gas called carbon dioxide. Keeping up a constant supply of oxygen and always getting rid of the carbon dioxide is necessary for cells to stay alive.

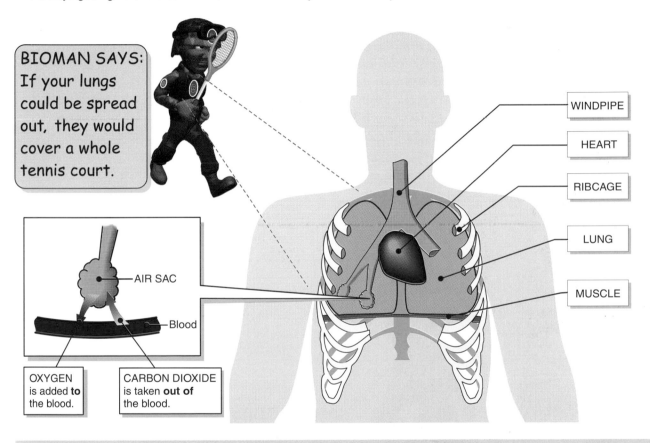

BIOMAN SAYS:
If your lungs could be spread out, they would cover a whole tennis court.

AIR SAC

Blood

OXYGEN is added **to** the blood.

CARBON DIOXIDE is taken **out of** the blood.

WINDPIPE

HEART

RIBCAGE

LUNG

MUSCLE

Exercise 3.1: Heart and lungs

1. Draw a simple diagram to show how blood circulates in our bodies. Label the organs and put arrows to show the direction of the blood flow to and from the heart.

2. Why do we need a circulation?

3. Why is it important that there is elastic material in the walls of the lungs?

Extension question

4. (a) A typical pulse rate is about 75 beats per minute. How many times does your heart beat in 1 hour?

    (b) Each beat of the heart pushes out about 70cm3 of blood. How much blood is pumped out every hour?

Exercise and the heart

Things to think about

- By now we should know that any living organism needs a supply of food and oxygen, and that these substances provide the energy needed to keep the cells alive.
- The heart acts as a pump to move blood around the body, and the blood contains food and oxygen which it delivers to the cells.
- The muscles of the body are responsible for movement.

When an animal moves, it needs energy to do so. The movement could be as simple as lifting an arm up and down, or as energetic as running a marathon. Indeed any amount of exercise will mean that the muscle cells need to be given more energy.

Energy is provided by food and oxygen. There is a kind of 'burning' process that lets out the energy that is stored in food. During exercise more and more energy is needed, so more food and oxygen must be delivered to the muscle cells. The way this happens is shown in the diagram below:

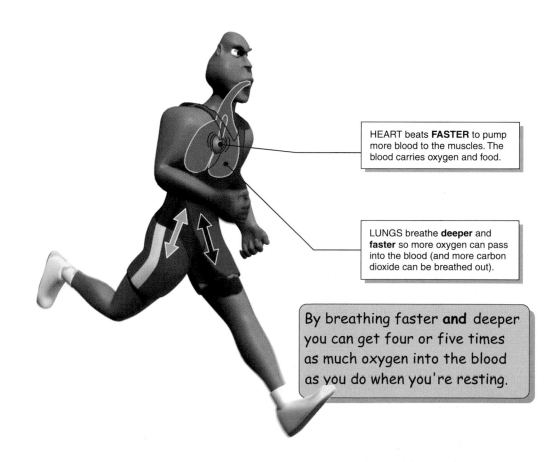

HEART beats **FASTER** to pump more blood to the muscles. The blood carries oxygen and food.

LUNGS breathe **deeper** and **faster** so more oxygen can pass into the blood (and more carbon dioxide can be breathed out).

By breathing faster **and** deeper you can get four or five times as much oxygen into the blood as you do when you're resting.

Measuring exercise

As you exercise, the heart has to beat faster and faster to pump more blood around the body. Your pulse rate changes during exercise; it rises when you are doing a lot and begins to return to normal when you stop. In fit people the pulse rate is slower than normal when they are at rest (i.e. not exercising), and after exercise it returns to normal much more quickly. You can measure the changes in your pulse rate during and after excercise as shown below.

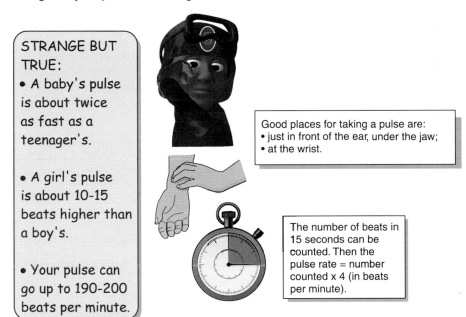

STRANGE BUT TRUE:
• A baby's pulse is about twice as fast as a teenager's.

• A girl's pulse is about 10-15 beats higher than a boy's.

• Your pulse can go up to 190-200 beats per minute.

Good places for taking a pulse are:
• just in front of the ear, under the jaw;
• at the wrist.

The number of beats in 15 seconds can be counted. Then the pulse rate = number counted x 4 (in beats per minute).

Is exercise good for you?

Remember that the heart is made of muscle and because exercise makes the heart beat faster it actually increases the 'fitness' of the heart muscle. This means that regular exercise gives you a 'fitter' heart and you are much less likely to suffer a heart attack if you take regular exercise.

Exercise benefits your health in other ways too:

● It **reduces obesity** because it uses up food reserves. Obesity (when you are so overweight that your health is affected) can be very harmful. For example, the extra weight can cause damage to your joints.

● It **increases stamina** because it trains the heart and lungs to deliver more oxygen to the working muscle cells. This means that when you need to exercise for long periods you will be able to do it without harming yourself.

● It **increases strength** because the muscles are being trained. Different types of exercise can provide extra strength in different muscles. Lifting weights and swimming is good for the arms, whereas running is more likely to benefit the legs.

As well as exercise, there are other ways in which you can have a healthy lifestyle. Some of these are described on page 33.

BIOMAN SAYS:
Most people who exercise regularly (at least three times a week) will notice a difference in strength and stamina after just four weeks.

MORE STRENGTH: The more work that the muscles do, the stronger they become.

MORE STAMINA: Exercise means that you can keep working for longer without becoming tired.

LESS OBESITY: Exercise 'burns up' food stores and reduces the chance of becoming overweight.

Exercise 3.2: Exercise

1. Bioman went to the doctor for a check-up. The doctor listened to his heart with a stethoscope.

   (a) Where did the doctor place the end of the stethoscope to listen to his heart? Draw a simple diagam.

   (b) Which of the following is the most likely number of beats per minute that the doctor heard?

   | 17 | 71 | 717 | 7,717 |

2. The doctor then took Bioman's pulse. Explain how he did this.

3. The doctor then asked Bioman whether he took much exercise. Why does exercise make your heart beat faster and your lungs breathe deeper?

Extension question

4. A pupil had his heart rate (pulse rate) measured every five minutes for a period of an hour. The results are shown in this table:

Time (minutes)	0	5	10	15	20	25	30	35	40	45	50	55	60
Pulse rate (beats per minute)	72	72	75	90	107	124	127	111	90	76	72	72	72

   (a) Plot a graph of the results (you may wish to do this on a computer). Put time on the horizontal axis (i.e. along the bottom) and pulse rate on the vertical axis (i.e. up the side). Give your graph a suitable title.

   (b) From the graph try to work out:
   - i. the resting heart rate;
   - ii. when the pupil began to take exercise;
   - iii. when the pupil stopped exercising;
   - iv. how long the pupil's pulse took to return to normal.

   (c) Why did the pulse rate increase during exercise?

Chapter 4
Humans are vertebrates

It's worth remembering

- One characteristic of living organisms is that they can move.
- Animals move by using muscles to pull on bones.
- Animals have many delicate internal organs, such as the brain and heart.

All living things can be classified into groups. They are classified according to special features which they have (see page 50). One of the features of animals is a bony skeleton, including a backbone made up of a series of small bones. Animals with a backbone are called **vertebrates**. Humans, like other vertebrates, have an *internal* skeleton which is the hard, bony material on the *inside* and softer muscle on the *outside*. The human skeleton does many things, some of which are shown below:

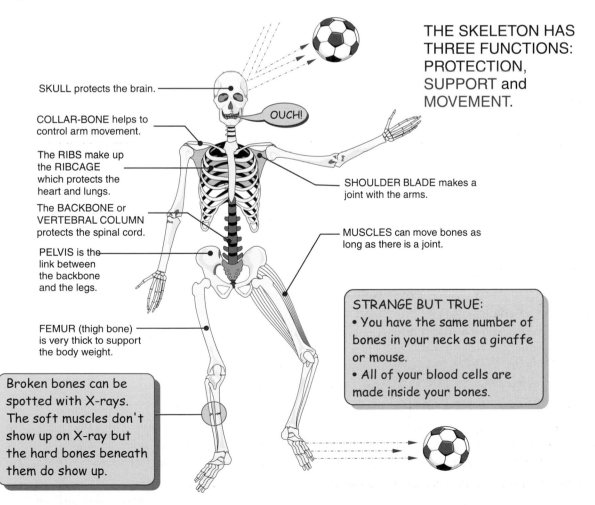

THE SKELETON HAS THREE FUNCTIONS: PROTECTION, SUPPORT and MOVEMENT.

SKULL protects the brain.

COLLAR-BONE helps to control arm movement.

The RIBS make up the RIBCAGE which protects the heart and lungs.

The BACKBONE or VERTEBRAL COLUMN protects the spinal cord.

PELVIS is the link between the backbone and the legs.

FEMUR (thigh bone) is very thick to support the body weight.

OUCH!

SHOULDER BLADE makes a joint with the arms.

MUSCLES can move bones as long as there is a joint.

STRANGE BUT TRUE:
- You have the same number of bones in your neck as a giraffe or mouse.
- All of your blood cells are made inside your bones.

Broken bones can be spotted with X-rays. The soft muscles don't show up on X-ray but the hard bones beneath them do show up.

Muscles, bones and movement

Although the skeleton has to be very hard, it must also be flexible to allow movement. Movement is possible because of the joints in our bodies where two bones meet. At these joints, muscles contract (i.e. get shorter) and pull the bones around the joint.

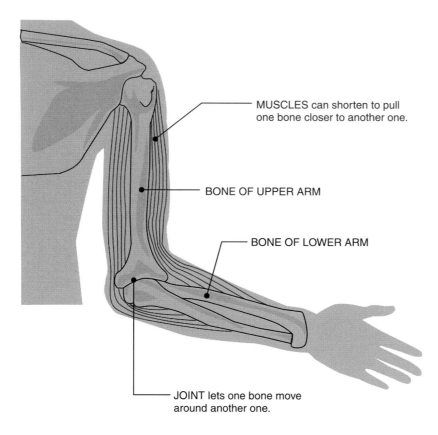

MUSCLES can shorten to pull one bone closer to another one.

BONE OF UPPER ARM

BONE OF LOWER ARM

JOINT lets one bone move around another one.

Four-legged vertebrates

We humans can stand on two legs, but most land vertebrates stand on four legs. Their skeletons are a little different from the human skeleton, but almost all of the same bones are there. The diagram opposite shows the skeleton of a horse and of a crocodile. You can clearly see how cleverly the bones are arranged in a way that suits each creature.

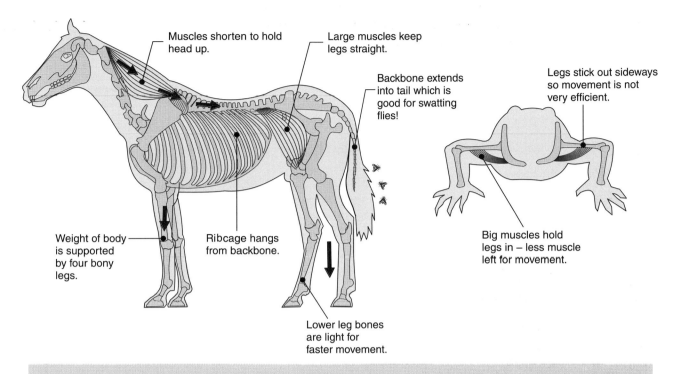

Muscles shorten to hold head up.

Large muscles keep legs straight.

Backbone extends into tail which is good for swatting flies!

Legs stick out sideways so movement is not very efficient.

Weight of body is supported by four bony legs.

Ribcage hangs from backbone.

Big muscles hold legs in – less muscle left for movement.

Lower leg bones are light for faster movement.

Exercise 4.1: The skeleton

1. Match the words in the first column with the phrases in the second column:

Bone	An animal with a backbone
Muscle	The mineral needed for strong bones
Skull	Protects the heart and lungs
Ribcage	Protects the brain
Pelvis	A hard substance that makes up the skeleton
Collar-bone	Has a joint for the arm
Shoulder blade	The soft tissue that shortens to move a bone
Joint	The link between the backbone and the legs
Calcium	Protects the spinal cord
Vertebrate	Stops your arm from going too far backwards
Backbone	A place where two bones meet

Extension question

2. (a) When Bioman fell off his motorbike, the doctor suggested that he should have an X-ray. Why is an X-ray used to check for a broken bone?

   (b) Bioman suspected that his older sister was pregnant when he noticed that she was drinking more milk than usual. Why are pregnant women advised to drink more milk?

Chapter 5
The human life cycle: how humans change as they grow

Important information

- One of the characteristics of living organisms is that they can reproduce.

- All living organisms are able to grow.

A human baby is produced by combining special cells from its mother and father. The mother and father cannot make these special cells until they are mature, and it takes about nine months from the joining of these special cells until the baby is born. It then takes many years for the baby to grow into an adult person.

There are several stages of development that humans go through from birth to old age. We can recognise each of these stages by certain special features. These are described in the diagram below:

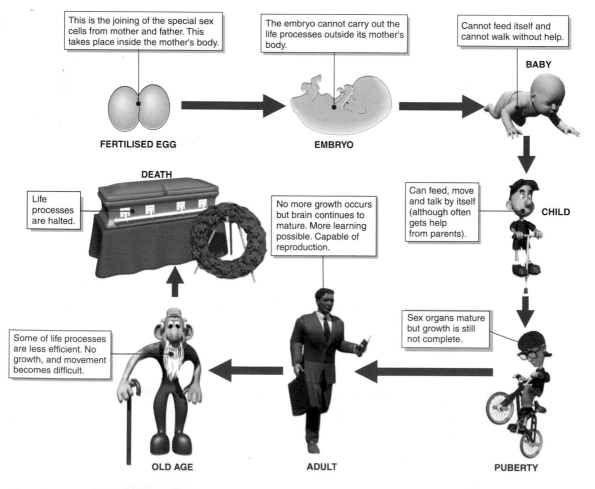

This is the joining of the special sex cells from mother and father. This takes place inside the mother's body.

The embryo cannot carry out the life processes outside its mother's body.

Cannot feed itself and cannot walk without help.

BABY

FERTILISED EGG

EMBRYO

DEATH

Life processes are halted.

No more growth occurs but brain continues to mature. More learning possible. Capable of reproduction.

Can feed, move and talk by itself (although often gets help from parents).

CHILD

Some of life processes are less efficient. No growth, and movement becomes difficult.

Sex organs mature but growth is still not complete.

OLD AGE

ADULT

PUBERTY

Puberty

One of the most important changes in the life cycle of a human is called puberty. At puberty the body begins to change from the body of a child to the body of an adult. In particular, the parts of the body that will allow the young person to reproduce now develop. Some of the changes that take place occur inside the body and some of the changes occur on the outside of the body. Some of these changes are shown below:

IN A GIRL:
• breasts develop
• hips widen
• periods begin

IN BOTH BOYS AND GIRLS:
• body grows rapidly
• pubic hair begins to grow

IN A BOY:
• voice gets deeper
• testes and penis grow
• muscles develop

BIOMAN SAYS (in a deep voice):
Puberty usually occurs one or two years later in boys than in girls.

Exercise 5.1: Development

1. Below is a list of the stages of development that humans go through. Match up the stages in the first column with the descriptions in the second column.

Childhood   No further growth, but brain continues to mature

Old age   Body functions slow down

Puberty   Life processes have stopped

Infancy (still a baby)   Not able to feed without help from parents

Embryo   Learning to walk and talk

Toddler   Able to talk, walk and feed itself

Death   Sex organs have become mature

Adulthood   Cannot carry out the life processes outside the mother's body

2. Put the stages from question 1 into the correct order, starting with the embryo.

3. (a) Describe which of the life stages above you are at.

   (b) Give a reason for your answer to (a).

   (c) Which life stage is your mother/father at?

   (d) Give a reason for your answer to (c).

Extension question

4. This table shows the average height of a group of boys from birth to 18 years of age.

Age in years	0	2	4	6	8	10	12	14	16	18
Height in cm	50	80	105	120	125	130	150	160	171	180

   (a) Plot a line graph of the results.

   (b) How old is a boy before he is three times his height at birth?

Chapter 6
Healthy living

- A living organism can carry out life processes.
- During the human life cycle growth and development of both body and brain takes place.
- A human life ends when the person is no longer able to carry out the life processes.

The human body is very good at carrying out life processes, and can stay alive despite many problems. However, for a human to stay fit and keep healthy there should be:

- a balanced diet (see page 19);
- a regular amount of exercise (see page 24); and
- no unnecessary health risks.

Taking health risks can seriously damage the body and the brain

CIGARETTES: Smoking cigarettes can make breathing very difficult. If smoking continues for a long time, there is a high risk of heart disease and lung cancer.

SOLVENTS and AEROSOLS: These are abused by sniffing and breathing in fumes. Glues and paint can damage the brain, and aerosols can cause a person to choke and suffocate.

DRUGS: Any chemical that affects the way the body works is a drug. Some drugs are useful, but many others are dangerous. Some can damage the brain, some can make the stomach bleed and others can make the liver stop working. Many drugs sold by drug dealers are not pure, and the impurities can make people very ill.

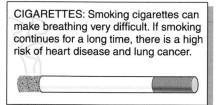

ALCOHOL: Alcohol is a very dangerous drug. In small amounts it slows down your reactions, and may cause you to lose a lot of your body heat. In larger amounts, alcohol damages the liver, stomach and the heart. It also makes people put on weight and can damage the sex organs.

WHAT IS ADDICTION? Many people become addicted to drugs. This means that they can't carry on their normal lives without the drug. It may mean that drug addicts will steal from their friends, and may go without food to buy drugs. Drug addicts who use needles can also catch blood diseases from needles they share with other drug addicts.

BIOMAN SAYS: Don't forget that even without these health risks you will need to eat a balanced diet and to take regular exercise.

Humans are not all the same. The differences between us could have been inherited from our parents, or they could be the result of our environment. Some of the differences may lead to an obvious disease, although others may just make us less healthy than we could be. We can do nothing about differences we inherit from our parents, but we can be careful about our lifestyle. Some of these lifestyle risks are described in the diagram on the previous page.

The most important point about these health risks is that **you have control over them**. You can make a choice about your lifestyle and remember that, when you read this, you have probably only lived one-seventh of your lifespan! It is possible that even a few uses of drugs can make you become addicted. What you choose to do as you grow up could affect the rest of your life, and the lives of your friends and relatives.

Exercise 6.1: Healthy living

1. Make a list of the three requirements for a healthy lifestyle.

2. What are the seven components that make up a balanced diet?

3. Name three benefits of regular exercise.

4. Bioman's uncle is a heavy smoker. Why does he find it difficult to exercise?

5. (a) Bioman has an obese cousin called Henry who eats a lot of fatty foods. Suggest why it is unhealthy to eat too many fatty foods.

   (b) Suggest two lifestyle changes that Bioman's obese cousin could make to become more healthy.

6. Match up the following features of lifestyle with the problems they cause:

Smoking	Weakness of muscles
Excessive use of alcohol	Damage to the liver
Addiction to drugs	Obesity
Over-eating of fatty foods	Choking to death
Too little exercise	Poor brain development
Breathing aerosols	Lung cancer

Chapter 7
The life of plants: nutrition

- Plants are living organisms, and can carry out life processes.

- Plants must be able to make food because the food provides raw materials for growth as well as energy.

- Plants do not move very much, so they must be able to feed themselves without moving.

Green plants make food using sunlight

Very few plants can trap or catch ready-made food. Instead they must make their own food. They make their food by combining **carbon dioxide gas** from the air with **water** and **nutrients** from the soil. They need energy to do this and this **energy** comes from the **sunlight**. This 'sun' energy is trapped by a green pigment in the leaves of the plant.

The method plants use to feed themselves is called **photosynthesis** and in fact the name gives you a clue to what happens during this process.

> BIOMAN SAYS: Don't be worried by long names in science - often a word can be easier to understand if it's broken down into smaller parts:

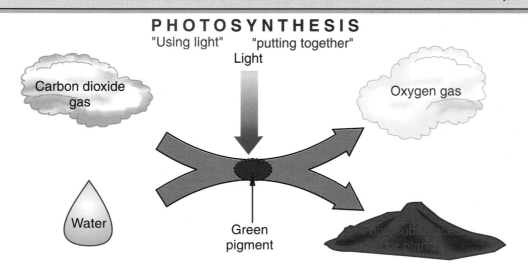

PHOTOSYNTHESIS
"Using light"   "putting together"
Light

Carbon dioxide gas

Oxygen gas

Water

Green pigment

You can see that the process of photosynthesis provides **food** for the plant, and also releases the gas **oxygen**. Animals depend on plants because they need to breathe oxygen, so that they can release the energy out of their food. Remember the example of working muscles (see page 24). Oxygen is also needed by animals, so that when they eat *plants,* any stored food that the plant has made can be used to provide energy for the animal. Equally, plants depend on animals because plants need the carbon dioxide gas that animals produce when they use energy from food, so that they can photosynthesise (or photosynthetise). And so the merry cycle continues! Quite simply, plants need animals and animals need plants. That's why it's so important that we protect the plant life on our planet. The diagram below shows how these two gases help to make animals and plants depend on each other.

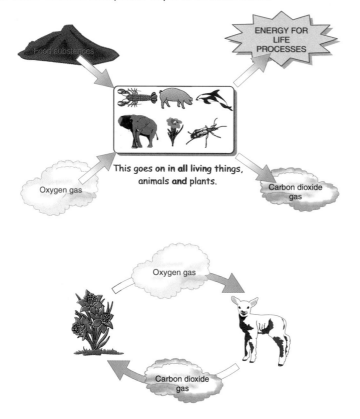

Any food that the plant has left over, after it has used some for energy, can be used for growing. The plant will be able to grow so long as it gets:

- **air** to provide carbon dioxide;
- **water** which is needed to combine with carbon dioxide, and to carry foods around the plant's body;
- **light** to provide the energy needed to join carbon dioxide and water together (photosynthesis); and
- a **suitable temperature**, so that all the chemical reactions in the plant can happen at the right rate.

Checking how factors affect plant growth

Scientists are very interested in how different factors affect plant growth. If they can understand how plants grow, then they may be able to make plants grow more quickly. This could provide more food for humans and other animals.

When a scientist has an idea that he or she wants to check, then he will need to carry out an **experiment**. The experiment must be reliable, or the information it gives will be useless. Our scientist below shows us how to design a reliable experiment.

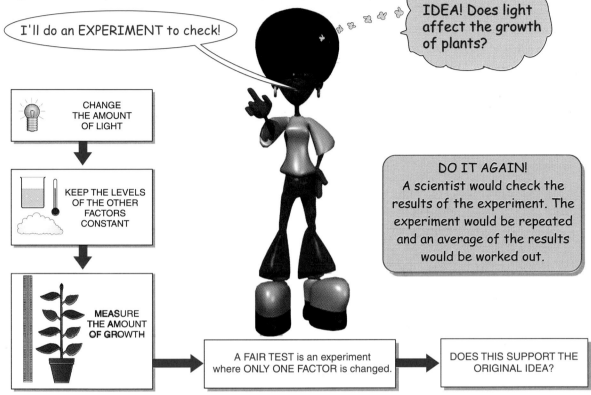

There are different ways that the **growth** of the plant could be measured. The **length** of the plant could be measured, or the plant could be **weighed**. If the scientist wanted to check how a change in temperature, light, water or carbon dioxide affected the growth of the plant, it would be necessary to use many plants. Different tests could be carried out at the same time on different plants that all started out being the same size at the beginning of the experiment.

Exercise 7.1: Plant nutrition

Study the diagram above and then complete this table to show that you understand the idea of a fair test.

Factors to be varied	Factors to be measured	Factors to be kept constant
Light	Length of plant	
Amount of carbon dioxide	Length of plant	
Amount of water	Length of plant	
Temperature	Length of plant	

Leaves and roots help plants to grow

Remember

- Plants make food during a process called photosynthesis.
- Photosynthesis needs light and carbon dioxide.

We have learnt so far that plants feed themselves by using **light** to convert carbon dioxide and water into food. It is quite easy to see therefore that trapping light becomes a very important task for a plant. It shouldn't be a surprise then to find out that a lot of the plant's structure is very well adapted to this 'trapping' process.

CARBON DIOXIDE + WATER

FOOD + OXYGEN

GREEN LEAF:
- photosynthesis goes on here;
- green pigment absorbs light energy;
- leaf is thin and flat to trap light and carbon dioxide.

STEM:
- holds leaves up to the sun;
- carries food and water around the plant.

This OXYGEN is needed by all living organisms to 'burn up' food for energy.

I never knew plants were so cool!

WATER

ROOT:
- absorbs water and minerals;
- produces many smaller roots to spread out through the soil.

Earthworms' burrows make it easier for roots to spread through the soil.

The roots also **anchor** the plant, holding it firmly in the soil.

MINERALS   **MINERALS**

Plants and minerals

By now we all know that plants can make their own food by the process of photosynthesis. But that is not enough; they also need some mineral nutrients just as humans do. The plants suck up their mineral nutrients which are dissolved in water, from the soil using their roots. If the soil does not have enough of these mineral nutrients, the plant will not grow properly. Farmers can test the soil to see if there are enough minerals for their crops to grow. If the minerals are in short supply, the farmer can add fertilisers. A **fertiliser** usually contains all of the main minerals that a plant needs.

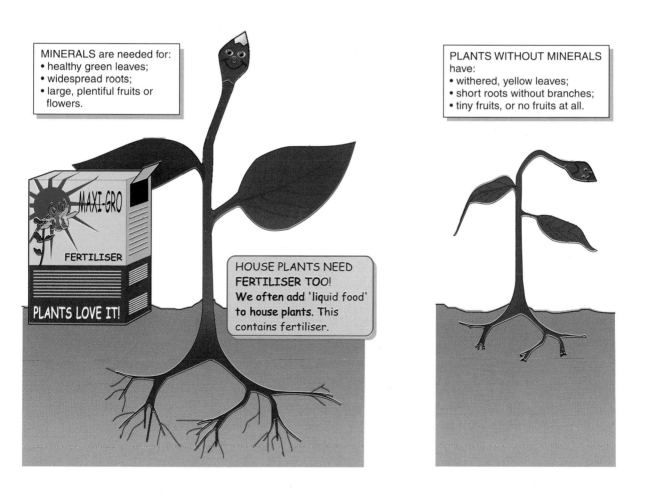

MINERALS are needed for:
• healthy green leaves;
• widespread roots;
• large, plentiful fruits or flowers.

PLANTS WITHOUT MINERALS have:
• withered, yellow leaves;
• short roots without branches;
• tiny fruits, or no fruits at all.

MAXI-GRO
FERTILISER
PLANTS LOVE IT!

HOUSE PLANTS NEED FERTILISER TOO!
We often add 'liquid food' to house plants. This contains fertiliser.

Plants and animals

Plants can produce food as long as they have a supply of carbon dioxide, water, light energy and minerals. They break down some of the food they make to release energy for their life processes. Any extra food they make they can use for growing purposes as we have already learnt, or they can **store** it in their bodies. This stored food provides animals with a useful food supply which is why many animals eat plants. Sometimes the animal eats the whole plant, or sometimes it may just steal the food store.

Plants are the only living organisms that can make their own food in this way. One way or another, all animals depend on plants for their food. This will be studied more in a later section (page 76 – food chains).

A squirrel steals plant food stored in a nut.

Exercise 7.2: Plant nutrition

1. (a) Draw a simple diagram of a plant, labelling the stem, leaves and roots.
   (b) What two jobs does the stem perform?
   (c) Why does a plant need roots?
   (d) What is the main job of a leaf? Give two ways in which the leaf is well adapted for this job.
2. Bioman has recently spent a lot of time in his garden, but his plants have not been growing very well. Suggest four reasons why a plant might not grow very well.

Extension question

3. Five sets of plants were grown. Each one had a slightly different treatment. The plants were weighed after two weeks of growth. How they were treated and how they grew is shown in the table below.

Treatment	Ideal conditions for air, water, light and minerals	Ideal conditions for air, water and light but only half the minerals	Ideal conditions for air, water and minerals, but only half the light	Ideal conditions for water, light and minerals but only half the amount of air	Ideal conditions for air, light and minerals, but only half the amount of water
Weight in grams	34	32	18	28	19

(a) Plot the results on a bar chart.
(b) Which treatment had the greatest effect on the plants' growth?
(c) Explain why this treatment had such an effect on the plants.

The life of the plant: reproduction

Starting point

- Plants make food by photosynthesis.
- Under the correct conditions of air, water, light and temperature a plant can grow.

An individual plant, like any other living organism, eventually dies. For a particular *species* of plant to survive, the *individual* plants of that species must be able to reproduce themselves. This process of **reproduction** is needed as part of the life cycle of a plant. The life cycle of a flowering plant is shown in the diagram below. Look at the different stages of the life cycle, and see how each stage leads on to the next one.

The life cycle of a flowering plant

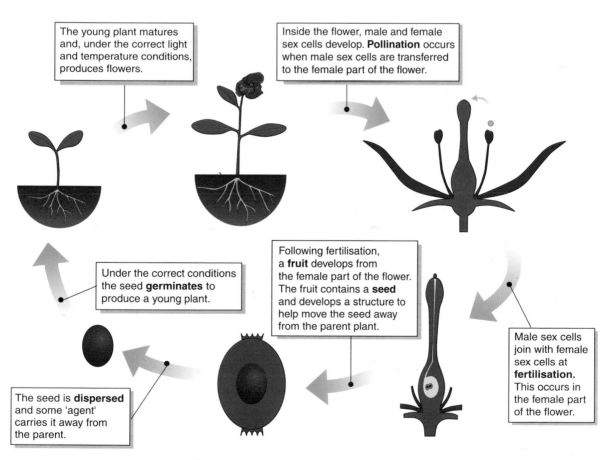

The young plant matures and, under the correct light and temperature conditions, produces flowers.

Inside the flower, male and female sex cells develop. **Pollination** occurs when male sex cells are transferred to the female part of the flower.

Under the correct conditions the seed **germinates** to produce a young plant.

Following fertilisation, a **fruit** develops from the female part of the flower. The fruit contains a **seed** and develops a structure to help move the seed away from the parent plant.

Male sex cells join with female sex cells at **fertilisation.** This occurs in the female part of the flower.

The seed is **dispersed** and some 'agent' carries it away from the parent.

The structure of flowers

A flower comes from a bud which is found at the end of a flower stalk. The flower is made up of **petals** which surround the special part of the plant that make the sex cells. The petals are usually the most obvious part of the flower. They often have bright colours and a pleasant smell. It is these two features that help the flower attract insects. Insects can be very important in transferring the sex cells between different flowers. We'll see why this is important in the next section.

There are two parts of the flower that actually make the sex cells. In the centre of the flower the **carpel** can be found. This is the female part of the flower. The female sex cells called **ovules** are made in the **ovary** at the bottom of the carpel. The male parts of the flower are the **stamens** and they grow in a circle around the carpel. The male sex cells, known as the **pollen,** are made in the **anthers** at the top of the stamens.

It's probably easier to understand the structure of an insect-pollinated flower from the picture below:

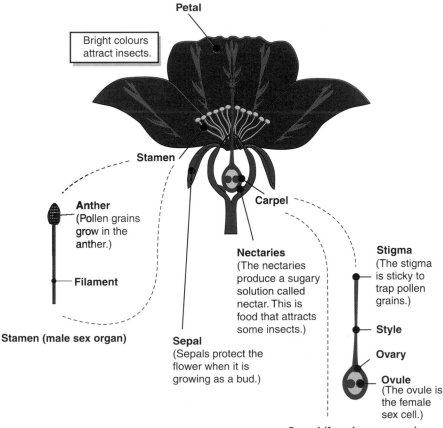

Petal

Bright colours
attract insects.

Stamen

Carpel

Anther
(Pollen grains
grow in the
anther.)

Filament

Stamen (male sex organ)

Sepal
(Sepals protect the
flower when it is
growing as a bud.)

Nectaries
(The nectaries
produce a sugary
solution called
nectar. This is
food that attracts
some insects.)

Stigma
(The stigma
is sticky to
trap pollen
grains.)

Style

Ovary

Ovule
(The ovule is
the female
sex cell.)

Carpel (female sex organ)

There are many different types of flower. They are different from each other because the pollination stage in the life cycle of the plant can be carried out in different ways. We will learn about these on page 44.

Exercise 7.3: Plant reproduction

1. Match the parts of a flower in the left-hand column with the correct function from the right-hand column.

Flower parts	Functions	
(a) pollen	1.	supports the anther
(b) flower stalk	2.	make a sweet, sugary solution
(c) style	3.	contains the female sex cells
(d) filament	4.	protects the flower in bud
(e) anther	5.	delivers the male sex cells
(f) stigma	6.	forms a base for the flower
(g) petal	7.	holds up the stigma
(h) nectaries	8.	attracts insects
(i) ovary	9.	produces pollen
(j) sepal	10.	receives pollen

2. Draw a simple diagram of an insect-pollinated flower, labelling all the flower parts from the list above.

3. Complete the paragraph below about reproduction in plants. Use words from this list:

DISPERSAL

REPRODUCTION

GERMINATES

POLLINATION

FRUIT

FERTILISATION

SEED

FLOWER

The life cycle of a flowering plant has a number of stages. A young plant develops when a seed ....
The plant matures until it produces a .... which has several parts adapted for ....
Male sex cells are transferred to the female part of the flower during the process of ....
These sex cells join with female sex cells at .... Following this process the ovary develops
into a .... This contains a .... and the method for moving it away from the
parent plant. This process which is called ...., requires some help to remove the seed
from the parent plant.

Pollination and fertilisation

The transfer of male sex cells to female sex cells is called pollination

This is the story so far:

- plants must be able to reproduce;
- the flowers are the reproductive part of the plant;
- stamens produce the male sex cells called pollen grains; and
- the carpel receives the male sex cells.

Individual plants cannot move very much at all. For sexual reproduction to occur, the male sex cells must be carried to the female part of the flower. This may be a very simple process, with the pollen just being transferred from the anther to the stigma of the same flower. However, it is better if the pollen grains can be carried to a different flower, so some 'helping hand' is needed to carry the pollen grains from the anthers of one flower to the stigma of another. This is most often an **insect** or the **wind**. The diagram below shows how an insect can carry pollen from one flower to another. This process is called **pollination**.

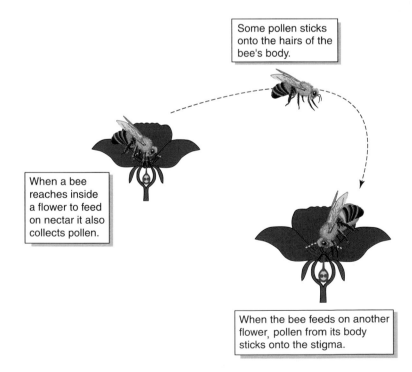

Some pollen sticks onto the hairs of the bee's body.

When a bee reaches inside a flower to feed on nectar it also collects pollen.

When the bee feeds on another flower, pollen from its body sticks onto the stigma.

Pollination is complete once the pollen from an anther has landed on the stigma of the same or another flower. The next step in the plant's life cycle is **fertilisation** which is when the male and female sex cells join together. This process goes on deep in the ovary of the flower.

Fertilisation

Here are some important points to learn about this part of the process.

- The male sex cell of a flower is inside the pollen grain and the female sex cell is inside the ovule.

- For fertilisation to take place the male sex cell in the pollen grain on the stigma must be able to reach the female sex cell, inside the ovule in the ovary;

- This is possible because a **pollen tube** grows out of the pollen grain when the grain lands on the surface of the stigma.

- The tube grows down through the style, through the ovary wall and eventually enters the ovule through a small hole.

- The male sex cell can then travel down the pollen tube, enter the ovule and join with the female sex cell.

This process is explained in the diagram below.

Fertilisation also starts the production of food stores inside the ovule. These food stores will be necessary for the development of the embryo and the early growth of the seedling, before the young plant is able to photosynthesise for itself.

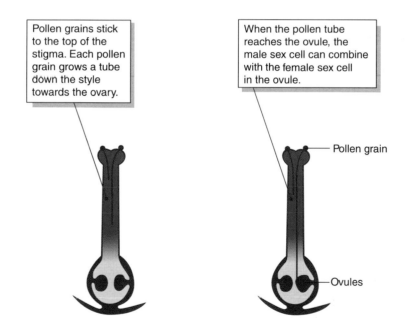

Pollen grains stick to the top of the stigma. Each pollen grain grows a tube down the style towards the ovary.

When the pollen tube reaches the ovule, the male sex cell can combine with the female sex cell in the ovule.

Pollen grain

Ovules

The formation of fruit and seed

After the male sex cell has joined with the female sex cell, the fertilised egg divides many times to produce an embryo. The **embryo** is made up of a tiny **shoot** and a tiny **root** together with two special leaves that can act as **food stores**. The outside of the ovule becomes hard to form a **seed coat**. Together the embryo and the seed coat make up a **seed**. The structure of a seed is shown in the diagram on the next page.

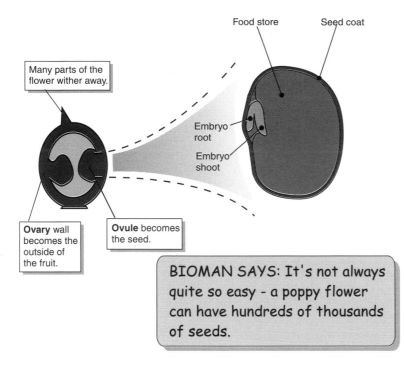

BIOMAN SAYS: It's not always quite so easy - a poppy flower can have hundreds of thousands of seeds.

After fertilisation, the seed sends messages to the flower. These messages make the flower change.

- The sepals and petals wither away, and may fall off.
- The stamens, stigma and style wither away.
- The wall of the ovary changes. Sometimes it becomes hard and dry, like a walnut; sometimes it becomes fleshy and juicy, like a plum; and it can even become tough and leathery, like a sunflower seed.

The ovary is now called a **fruit**. The fruit has the function of dispersing the seeds away from the parent plant (see opposite).

Exercise 7.4: Pollination and fertilisation

1. (a) What is the difference between pollination and fertilisation?
   (b) Explain the process of pollination.
   (c) Explain what happens during fertisation and draw a simple diagram to illustrate the process.

2. How does the structure of a flower help in pollination?

3. Make a simple diagram of a typical flower. On your diagram label:
   (a) the parts which fall off after fertilisation;
   (b) the parts which develop into a fruit.

Extension question

4. Which of the following are (a) fruits, (b) seeds or (c) neither fruit nor seed?

   Tomato, cucumber, sprout, baked bean, runner bean, celery, pea, grape.

Dispersal of seeds and fruits

Remember

- A seed is formed after fertilisation.
- The seed is inside the part of the flower that hasn't withered away.
- The seed and the ovary together make up the fruit.

The seed contains an embryo plant. Before it can develop into a new young plant the seed must be separated from its parent plant. The new young plant, like its parent, will need water, carbon dioxide and light to grow. If the young plant is too close to the parent, it will struggle to get enough of these essential substances. The parent plant develops a way of scattering the seeds, so that the young plants will be far enough away not to be a nuisance! This scattering is called **seed dispersal**. Fruits are adapted in many ways to help dispersal of the seeds, as the diagram below shows:

Dispersal of seeds

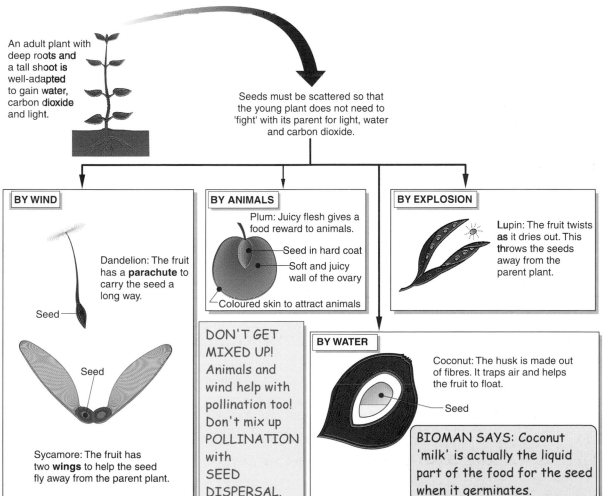

An adult plant with deep roots and a tall shoot is well-adapted to gain water, carbon dioxide and light.

Seeds must be scattered so that the young plant does not need to 'fight' with its parent for light, water and carbon dioxide.

BY WIND

Dandelion: The fruit has a **parachute** to carry the seed a long way.

Seed

Seed

Sycamore: The fruit has two **wings** to help the seed fly away from the parent plant.

BY ANIMALS

Plum: Juicy flesh gives a food reward to animals.

Seed in hard coat

Soft and juicy wall of the ovary

Coloured skin to attract animals

BY EXPLOSION

Lupin: The fruit twists **as** it dries out. This throws the seeds away from the parent plant.

DON'T GET MIXED UP! Animals and wind help with pollination too! Don't mix up POLLINATION with SEED DISPERSAL.

BY WATER

Coconut: The husk is made out of fibres. It traps air and helps the fruit to float.

Seed

BIOMAN SAYS: Coconut 'milk' is actually the liquid part of the food for the seed when it germinates.

Germination of seeds

Once the seeds are scattered, hopefully landing some distance away from the parent plant, the seed can begin to grow. Remember from the previous section, a seed is made up of a tiny new plant called an embryo plus a food store. If the seed can get enough **water**, **oxygen** and **warmth**, then the embryo begins to grow. This process is called **germination**. During the process of germination, the food stores inside the seed are used to make leaves and roots. Once the young plant has its own leaves and roots, it can begin making its own food by photosynthesis.

Germination of most seeds follows the same pattern.

Germination: A seed changes into a young plant

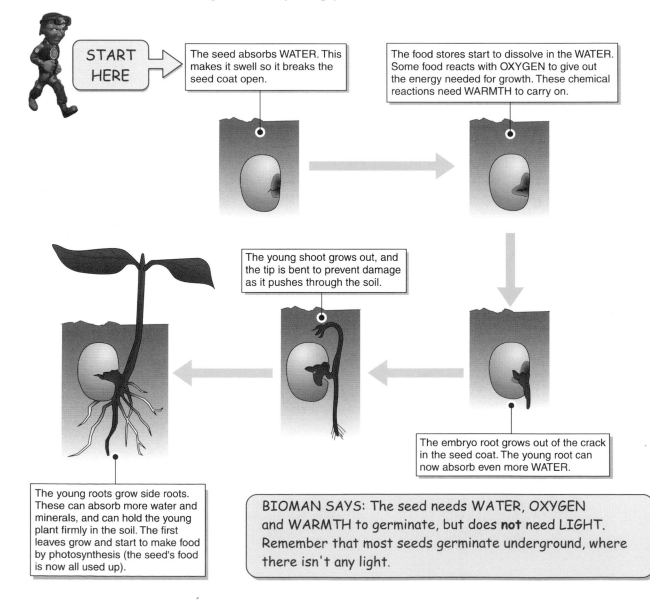

START HERE

The seed absorbs WATER. This makes it swell so it breaks the seed coat open.

The food stores start to dissolve in the WATER. Some food reacts with OXYGEN to give out the energy needed for growth. These chemical reactions need WARMTH to carry on.

The young shoot grows out, and the tip is bent to prevent damage as it pushes through the soil.

The embryo root grows out of the crack in the seed coat. The young root can now absorb even more WATER.

The young roots grow side roots. These can absorb more water and minerals, and can hold the young plant firmly in the soil. The first leaves grow and start to make food by photosynthesis (the seed's food is now all used up).

BIOMAN SAYS: The seed needs WATER, OXYGEN and WARMTH to germinate, but does **not** need LIGHT. Remember that most seeds germinate underground, where there isn't any light.

Exercise 7.5: Dispersal and germination

1. (a) Explain why seeds are dispersed away from their parent plant.

   (b) Describe three methods by which seeds can be dispersed.

2. Look at the diagram of the sycamore seed on page 47. Why is it suited to its method of dispersal?

3. Draw a diagram of a seed that would be suited to dispersal by a furry animal. Explain why it is suited to this method of dispersal.

4. Why are fruits such as cherries so brightly-coloured and sweet-tasting?

5. (a) Draw and label the main parts of a germinating runner bean.

   (b) Explain what a seed needs in order to germinate.

   (c) Why does a plant need roots?

   (d) Why does a plant need a stem?

   (e) Explain why the leaves of a plant stretch out towards the light.

   (f) What is it about a leaf that makes it good at capturing light energy?

   (g) Why does a plant need light energy?

6. Match up these parts of the seed with the job they carry out:

The embryo shoot	provides the first raw materials for the growth of the young plant.
The embryo root	grows into the stem and leaves.
The seed coat	grows to anchor the young plant in the soil and absorb water.
The food store	protects the embryo against drying out and rotting.

Chapter 8
Variation and classification

Here's a small reminder from Bioman of what we should know by now:

- All living organisms can carry out the seven life processes (growth, nutrition, reproduction, movement, excretion, respiration and sensitivity).

- Different organisms have different features that make them able to survive in different environments.

- Plants and animals feed themselves in very different ways.

The variety of living organisms

There are many differences between living organisms. These differences are called **variations**. Even humans show variations; they come in many different shapes, sizes and colours. Just imagine how many variations humans show in features such as eye colour, skin colour, shapes of earlobes and so on, and now think about how many variations there must be between humans and other species!

Scientists have found that there are millions of different species of animals and plants. Different species exist because different features exist. Scientists try to give each different species a special name. This helps them when they are trying talk to one another about different organisms. There are so many different species on Earth that no one person, not even Bioman, could possibly learn all of their names. It is impossible even to remember the names of all the different insects, and insects are only one group in the animal kingdom. This can be a great problem for scientists, or indeed for anyone interested in living things. It would be very difficult for you even to memorise the names of the organisms you might find on a trip to the seaside. Try it and see how many you can actually recall!

To overcome this problem scientists have developed a way of making **keys** as a short cut to identifying different species.

Using and making a key

A key is a set of questions that we can ask for ourselves. Each question should have two possible answers. The answer to one question leads on to another question. This goes on until the name of the organism is found.

One kind of key is called a **branching key** or **spider key**. Try to use this branching key to classify the organisms shown below:

Fig.1

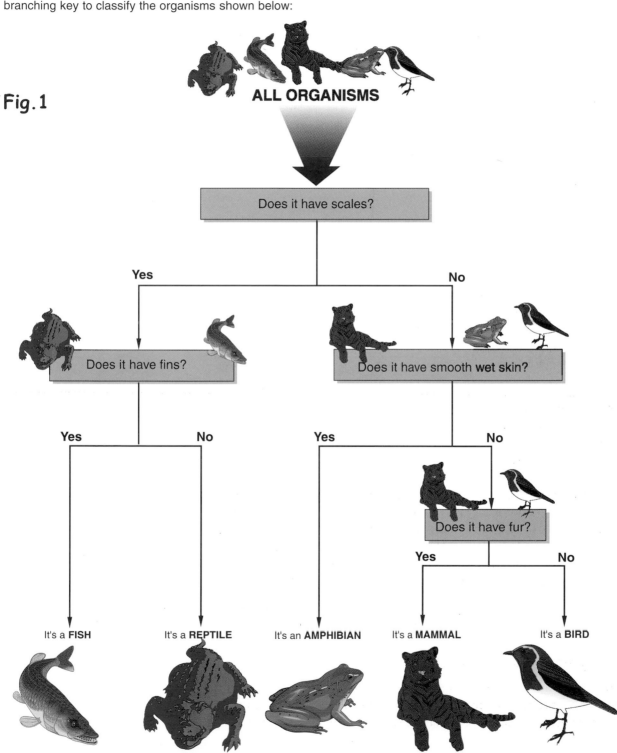

ALL ORGANISMS

Does it have scales?

Yes — No

Does it have fins?

Does it have smooth **wet skin**?

Yes — No   Yes — No

Does it have fur?

Yes — No

It's a **FISH**   It's a **REPTILE**   It's an **AMPHIBIAN**   It's a **MAMMAL**   It's a **BIRD**

The problem with branching keys is that they can take up a lot of space. The way to get around this problem is to use a **numbered key**. In a numbered key, each question is given a number. The answer to the question may send you to another number. Try making a numbered key to classify these creepy crawlies:

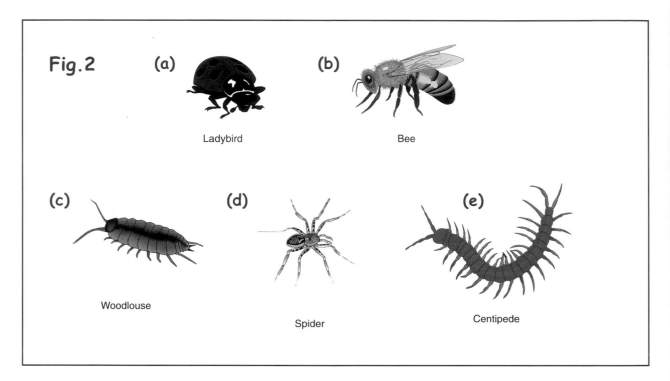

Fig.2

(a) Ladybird

(b) Bee

(c) Woodlouse

(d) Spider

(e) Centipede

KEY:

1.	Does it have 6 legs?	YES	Go to question 2.
		NO	Go to question 3.
2.	Does it have hard cases for its wings?	YES	It's a Ladybird.
		NO	It's a Bee.
3.	Does it have 8 legs?	YES	It's a Spider.
		NO	Go to question 4.
4.	Does it have more than 20 legs?	YES	It's a Centipede.
		NO	It's a Woodlouse.

Now try making another key. The way to do this for a group of organisms is to try to split the big group into smaller and smaller groups. It is very important that the questions you use to split the group up are sensible ones. For example, this group of organisms could be separated into two groups, those that live on land and those that do not. Unfortunately this would put the fir tree, the beetle and the cat into the same group when they are biologically very different from one another.

Fig.3

Try to choose questions that are:

● based on biological features;

● based on features that are easy to see.

Now look again at this group of organisms. A better starting point would be to make up two groups, one of **plants** and the other of **animals**. Then the animals could be divided into **with legs** and **without legs**. The **with legs** group would include the butterfly, the crab and the cat; the next grouping could be **with fur** or **without fur**. There are other questions that would be just as useful, but these are certainly better than the one about **lives on land** or **doesn't live on land**.

Exercise 8.1: Keys

1. Make a branching key to identify these 'individuals'.

2. Now use your branching key to make a numbered key for these 'individuals'.

3. Look again at the group of organisms in fig. 3 on page 53. Arrange them into groups that would let you make a key for identifying them.

Extension questions

4. Look at the 'Life in a freshwater pond' picture on pages 70-71. Make a numbered key that would help you to identify the plants and creatures living in this habitat.

5. Look at the 'oak woodland' picture on pages 72-73 and make a numbered key to identify the plants and creatures living in this habitat.

The variety of life

Don't forget

- Living organisms show variation which means there are differences between them.
- Scientists can use these differences to produce keys.

Putting living things into groups

As we have seen, a key is very useful for identifying living things. A key works by asking a set of questions about the features an organism has. The answers we give to the questions begin to split up a large group of living things into individual organisms.

Scientists can also use the answers to these questions to put living things into groups. For example, we can put all living organisms into one of two groups just by getting the answer to a single question.

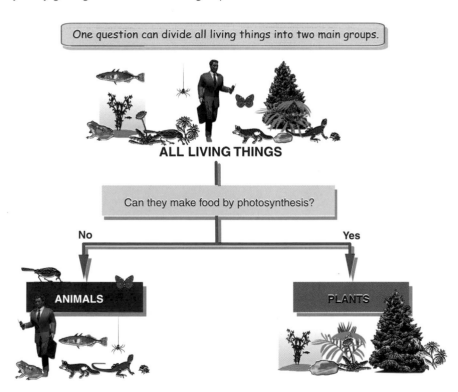

One question can divide all living things into two main groups.

ALL LIVING THINGS

Can they make food by photosynthesis?

No   Yes

ANIMALS   PLANTS

Scientists have been able to put all the known living organisms into groups by putting together all the organisms with similar features. This grouping together is called **classifying**.

All living organisms can be put into very large groups called **kingdoms**. There are five kingdoms but for the time being we only need to think about two of them, **animals** and **plants**.

The animal kingdom

All of the **animals** in the world can be put into one of two groups, either as a **vertebrate** or an **invertebrate**. We can put animals into the correct group by answering just one question.

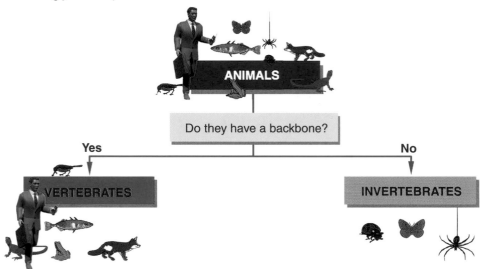

There are many times more invertebrates than vertebrates, but most of us recognise vertebrates more easily. There are five groups of **vertebrates** (animals with backbones). A good way of recognising the five groups is by looking at their skin.

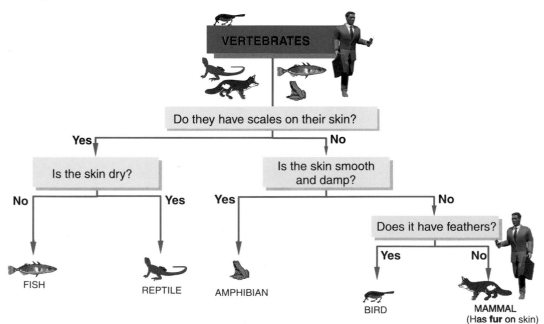

The invertebrates are animals without backbones. It's not always easy to tell that they haven't got backbones because some of them have very hard covers to their bodies.

Two of the invertebrate groups that have these hard body covers are the **insects** and the **spiders**. Some people think of them as all as just 'creepy-crawlies', but there are some important differences between these two groups.

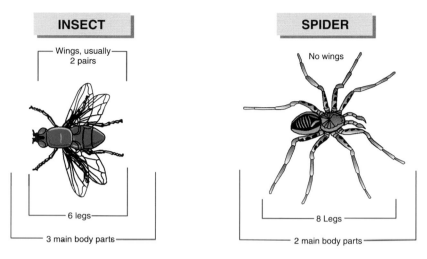

INSECT	SPIDER
Wings, usually 2 pairs	No wings
6 legs	8 Legs
3 main body parts	2 main body parts

The plant kingdom

All plants have one thing in common; they **all** have a pigment that can absorb light energy, so that they can make their own food by photosynthesis.

We can divide up all of the plants into two main groups, again by asking just one question.

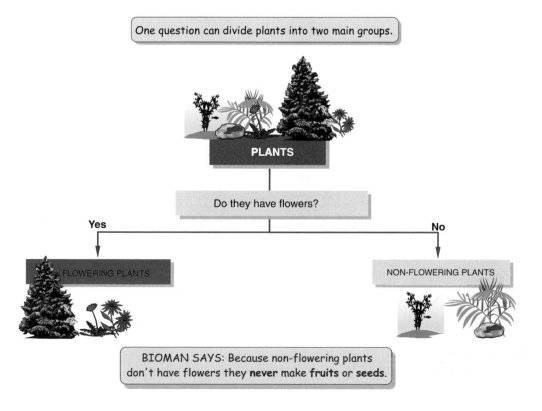

One question can divide plants into two main groups.

PLANTS

Do they have flowers?

Yes — FLOWERING PLANTS

No — NON-FLOWERING PLANTS

BIOMAN SAYS: Because non-flowering plants don't have flowers they **never** make **fruits** or **seeds**.

What is a species?

There are many other questions that can be asked to split these large groups into smaller and smaller groups. The smallest of all groups is called the **species**. Members of the same species are so much alike that males and females can mate and produce offspring just like themselves. Humans are one species, oak trees are another, barn owls are another and so on. Try to think of some others. Scientists have found that there are over five million species on Earth.

Exercise 8.2: The variety of life

1. Copy this table. Use information from this section to fill in the gaps. Put a ✓ if a feature is present and a ✗ if it is absent.

Feature	Fish	Amphibian	Reptile	Bird	Mammal
Backbone					
Scales					
Feathers					
Hairy skin					

2. Copy this table. Use information from this section to fill in the gaps. Put a ✓ if a feature is present and a ✗ if it is absent.

Feature	Insect	Spider
Eight legs		
Six legs		
Wings		
Three major body parts		
Two major body parts		

3. Give three examples of invertebrates. What feature makes each one an invertebrate?

4. Give three examples of vertebrates. What feature makes each one a vertebrate?

5. Give three examples of non-flowering plants and three examples of flowering plants. What feature is common to all plants?

Chapter 9
Protection of the environment

Remember

- Living things need their environments to have certain things in them.
- There is a great variety of life.

The environment is basically everything that surrounds a living organism. This includes things such as:

- other living organisms;
- the rocks and soil;
- the water;
- the air.

Here is an example of a living organism in its environment. The environment of a woodland can provide the sparrowhawk with food (small birds), shelter and a safe nesting site.

The part of the environment that a living organism lives in is called its **habitat**. The habitat has to provide a living organism with three things: enough food, proper shelter (from the cold, for example) and a safe place to breed. The organism may die, or have to move somewhere else, if the habitat does not provide these basic needs. The habitat might change, so that it doesn't provide these needs any longer. If that happens, then the variety of life in that piece of the environment will be reduced.

How can a habitat change?

A habitat can change naturally, but it can also change because of the activities of humans. We have all seen examples of natural changes, and some of these have probably been going on since the Earth was first formed. There have always been floods, volcanic eruptions and tremendous tropical storms. These natural disasters will have changed the habitat for many living organisms. Examples of these natural changes, and the effects they might have on living organisms, are shown in the next illustration. Here fire has destroyed a habitat.

Fire can cause natural changes to habitat

| Some mammals and birds can escape to undamaged habitat. | Plants and many insects and small mammals die because they cannot escape the flames. | Burned habitat is now very different for living organisms. |

Many scientists are much more worried about the effects that **humans** are having on the environment. Humans can affect the environment, and the living organisms in it, in three main ways:

- by **habitat destruction**, such as the cutting down of hedgerows to make fields bigger;
- by **pollution**, such as the burning of too many fossil fuels;
- by directly **killing** the living organisms, such as killing rhinos for their horns.

Habitat destruction is one of the main problems facing living organisms in Britain. Farmers have been cutting down hedges at the rate of 8 000 km per year for much of the last century. These hedges are cut down, so that there is more space to grow crops and use farm machinery, but living organisms can suffer. A well-grown hedge can provide nest sites for more than 60 species of birds, food for insects and fieldmice, and excellent shelter for animals moving from one wood to the next one.

Harsh cutting of hedges removes the habitat for wildlife.

Pollution creates a change to the environment caused by the activities of humans. We burn a lot of fuel because we need so much energy for our machines and so on. Burning fossil fuels such as coal and oil creates a lot of waste gases. These can affect the air, making it difficult to breathe, as well as adding acids to soil and water. These changes can be very harmful to living organisms.

Factories sometimes produce waste that can harm the environment.

Humans kill living organisms for many reasons. Sometimes this can be excused. Often, however, this killing cannot be excused, for example, when humans kill for sport, for fur or for products that they don't really need.

Poachers kill rhinos for their horns. Some people think that the horn contains powerful medicines, although scientists do not accept this idea.

Exercise 9.1: Damage to the environment

1. Look at the 'oak woodland' picture on pages 72-73.

    (a) Write down two natural ways in which this environment could change. Explain how this might affect the wildlife that lives there.

    (b) Write down two unnatural ways in which this environment could change.

2. Look at the 'freshwater pond' picture on pages 70-71.

    (a) Write down two natural ways in which this environment could change.

    (b) Write down two unnatural ways in which this environment could change. Explain how this might affect the wildlife that lives there.

Extension question

3. Find a newspaper, magazine or internet article that describes some damage to our environment. Write down three main things that the article says. Suggest action that could be taken to repair this damage.

Conservation

Humans may cause damage to the environment, but they can also do good things to the environment! Many people are now involved in **conservation**. Conservation involves looking for ways to protect the environment, and usually means that a balance, between what the humans take from the environment and what the wildlife requires, has been found.

There are many different kinds of conservation; a couple are described below.

- **Looking after the habitat.** This can involve protecting the habitat completely, perhaps by using fences to keep people and farm animals out. More trees can be planted and any plants that might take away light or water from the newly-planted trees can be cut down. Good nesting sites can be provided if there are no natural breeding places. A good example of this type of conservation is the way that some of Britain's rivers have been managed to help otters.

Saving otters

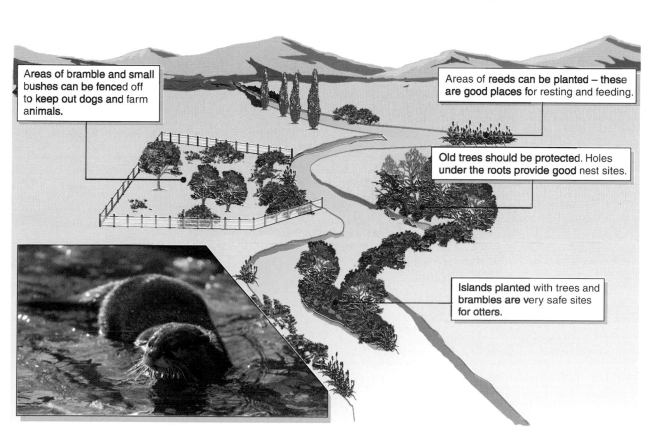

Areas of bramble and small bushes can be fenced off to keep out dogs and farm animals.

Areas of reeds can be planted – these are good places for resting and feeding.

Old trees should be protected. Holes under the roots provide good nest sites.

Islands planted with trees and brambles are very safe sites for otters.

● Another way is by **providing new habitats.** Wildlife conservation doesn't need to be 'in the wild'; we can actually do quite a lot for wildlife by making sure that our gardens provide the things that they need.

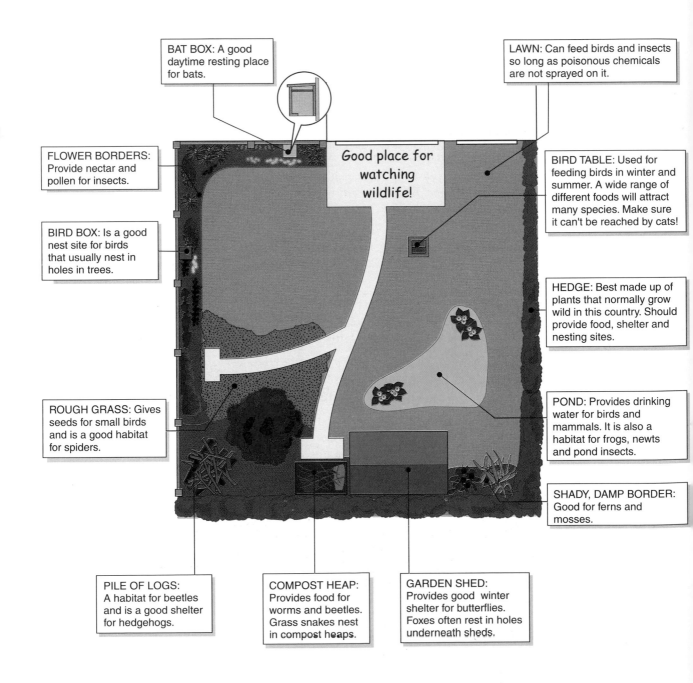

BAT BOX: A good daytime resting place for bats.

LAWN: Can feed birds and insects so long as poisonous chemicals are not sprayed on it.

FLOWER BORDERS: Provide nectar and pollen for insects.

Good place for watching wildlife!

BIRD TABLE: Used for feeding birds in winter and summer. A wide range of different foods will attract many species. Make sure it can't be reached by cats!

BIRD BOX: Is a good nest site for birds that usually nest in holes in trees.

HEDGE: Best made up of plants that normally grow wild in this country. Should provide food, shelter and nesting sites.

ROUGH GRASS: Gives seeds for small birds and is a good habitat for spiders.

POND: Provides drinking water for birds and mammals. It is also a habitat for frogs, newts and pond insects.

SHADY, DAMP BORDER: Good for ferns and mosses.

PILE OF LOGS: A habitat for beetles and is a good shelter for hedgehogs.

COMPOST HEAP: Provides food for worms and beetles. Grass snakes nest in compost heaps.

GARDEN SHED: Provides good winter shelter for butterflies. Foxes often rest in holes underneath sheds.

Britain is a small place, and the population is very high for a country of this size. This means that humans and wildlife will always be trying to get the same things from the land. The most important thing to remember about conservation is that it needs a **balance** between humans and wildlife.

Zoos and endangered species

Many animals are losing their wild habitat which can mean that they do not have enough food, or they may not have enough places to breed and raise their offspring. It can also mean that the wild animals have to look for food on farms or in villages. Because of this, some animals are becoming very rare and need human help if they are to survive. Humans can help by protecting the habitat, as we saw on the previous page, but this isn't always possible. Some animals can only be saved if they are kept in safe conditions in zoos.

Many people get a lot of pleasure from seeing wild animals in zoos, but other people think that the animals suffer from having to live in these unusual circumstances. Scientists often have to deal with questions like this, and some of the good and bad points about zoos are explained in the diagram below.

Good points

Animals get food and shelter and are looked after by a vet.

Animals may breed which is important in preserving endangered species.

People enjoy visiting zoos. Entry fees can be spent on animals' welfare and people may give money for conservation work.

Zoos may get people interested in animals and conservation.

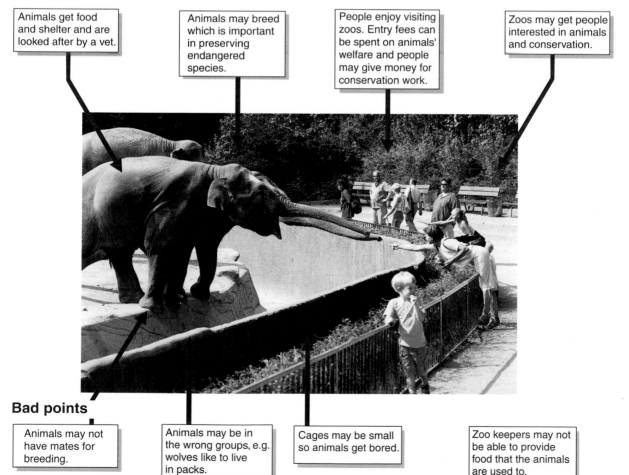

Bad points

Animals may not have mates for breeding.

Animals may be in the wrong groups, e.g. wolves like to live in packs.

Cages may be small so animals get bored.

Zoo keepers may not be able to provide food that the animals are used to.

Often the best solution would be to combine two things:

- firstly to work out the best way of breeding animals in zoos, so that the number of each species can be increased;

- and secondly to try to conserve some of the animal's natural habitat, so that the animals that are bred in zoos can eventually be returned to the wild.

Exercise 9.2: Conservation

1. Find a book about conservation or search on the internet for information about conservation projects. Find an example of (a) an animal, and (b) a plant in Britain that have been protected by conservation work.

2. Investigate the conservation work carried out by zoos. Describe three things that zoos are doing to help conserve endangered animals.

3. Give two ways in which a garden can be valuable for butterflies, and two ways it can be valuable for spiders.

Extension question

4. Design a pond that would provide a suitable habitat for wildlife. Name six creatures that might be attracted to this habitat.

Chapter 10
Adaptation

Adaptation means being well-suited to the environment.

- A habitat must provide a living organism with food, shelter and a breeding site.
- A habitat can change for many reasons.
- In our world such a huge variety of life exists because different organisms have different features.

Living organisms have features that let them survive in their environment. These features are called adaptations, and there are many different **adaptations** that allow living organisms to carry on with the life processes. These adaptations fall into different groups according to how they help the organism to survive (see page 11):

Feeding: Many animals have features that help them to feed efficiently. For example, hunting animals (predators – see page 77) often have sharp teeth and claws to kill prey, powerful muscles to chase them and very sensitive eyes to find them in the first place! Plants often have very large leaves to trap light and deep roots to reach water.

The cheetah is one of the most efficient hunters on the plains of Africa

Protection: Not all animals are hunters; some of them are chased by the hunters! These prey animals (see page 77) need to protect themselves. Some of them have a hard covering to their bodies.

The tortoise has a hard shell covering and protecting its body.

Some of them are coloured to blend into their background — they are **camouflaged**.

Can you spot the peppered moth on this lichen covered tree trunk?

Some animals have spines which can cause a huge amount of pain to any potential predators. Plants that live in dry environments often have a waxy covering to cut down the loss of water from their bodies, and spines to stop animals eating them.

Prickly hedgehogs

Movement: Whether an animal is a predator or a prey it will need to be able to move. There are many adaptations to make this possible. Birds have feathers that are light and give a big surface to help them fly. Fish are streamlined to 'cut' through the water, and camels have big flat feet, so that they can walk on sand without sinking.

'My big, flat feet are killing me!'

Day and night for living things

Most humans work and play during the day, and sleep at night. This isn't true for all animals; many of them come out at night. When they do this, we say that they are **nocturnal**. There are several reasons why they might only come out at night:

- They can feed on other animals that only come out at night. For example, many bats feed on moths and other insects that fly only when it's dark.
- They can avoid animals that feed during the day and because of this they won't be fighting over the same food. They can also hide from animals that might like to try to eat them.
- They can avoid the heat of the day in countries where it is very hot or in the desert, for example. This means they won't run the risk of drying out.

Nocturnal animals often have big eyes and very sensitive ears.

Living things and the seasons

A habitat must provide food, shelter and a nesting site. Sometimes a change in the environment might mean that a living organism can't get these three essential things from its habitat. Animals can do two things to deal with this problem.

Migration: Some animals simply go somewhere else where there is more food or where they won't need to shelter from the cold. These animals need three special adaptations that will allow them to escape the conditions they don't like:

- they must be able to move over long distances;
- they must be able to find their way, so that they don't get lost;
- they must be able to build up a food store to last them for the journey.

Birds are the champions as migrators. Swallows, for example, fly from England to South Africa in Autumn and then back again in Spring.

Hibernation: If an animal can't migrate, it may just cut down in its need for food by going to sleep! An animal that hibernates needs two main adaptations:

- it must be able to 'slow down' its life processes, so that it doesn't use up its food stores too quickly;
- it must be able to build up a food store which it usually does by laying down a lot of fat under its skin.

Of course, an animal that hibernates must be able to find a good shelter from the cold. In Britain, badgers, bats and squirrels hibernate. Polar bears hibernate for six months, and the females even have their babies while they are asleep!

The following diagrams of the pond and the oak woodland show some of the many ways living organisms are adapted to their habitats.

Life in a freshwater pond

MIGRATION (moving to another place), allows animals to find food during the winter. Migration is used by many birds (e.g. geese) and some mammals (e.g. reindeer).

The FROG has many survival features:
- it has a wide mouth to capture prey;
- it is camouflaged to avoid hunters;
- it is **nocturnal** to avoid hunters;
- it has webbed feet to help swimming;
- it has a sticky tongue to stretch out and catch insects.

The PLANT:
- has deep roots to anchor plant in mud;
- has a long stem to lift leaves out of water towards light.

BIOMAN SAYS: Sleep away the winter with HIBERNATION! Hibernation lets many animals survive the winter, when it's cold and **there isn't** much food.
- Animals (e.g. frogs, newts and many insects) find a hole and go to sleep.
- Because they are asleep they don't use up much energy.
- They wake up again in Spring when conditions are better.

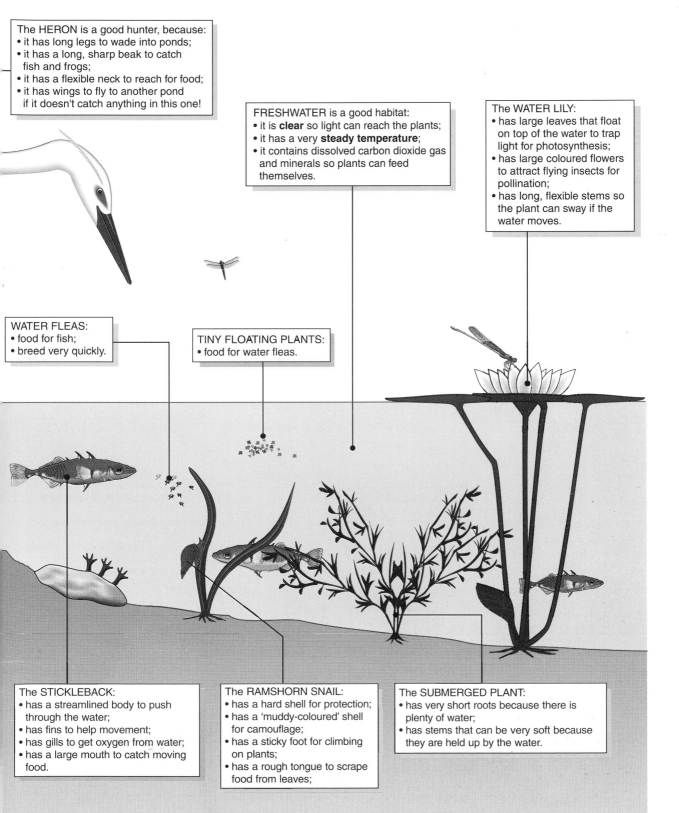

The HERON is a good hunter, because:
• it has long legs to wade into ponds;
• it has a long, sharp beak to catch fish and frogs;
• it has a flexible neck to reach for food;
• it has wings to fly to another pond if it doesn't catch anything in this one!

FRESHWATER is a good habitat:
• it is **clear** so light can reach the plants;
• it has a very **steady temperature**;
• it contains dissolved carbon dioxide gas and minerals so plants can feed themselves.

The WATER LILY:
• has large leaves that float on top of the water to trap light for photosynthesis;
• has large coloured flowers to attract flying insects for pollination;
• has long, flexible stems so the plant can sway if the water moves.

WATER FLEAS:
• food for fish;
• breed very quickly.

TINY FLOATING PLANTS:
• food for water fleas.

The STICKLEBACK:
• has a streamlined body to push through the water;
• has fins to help movement;
• has gills to get oxygen from water;
• has a large mouth to catch moving food.

The RAMSHORN SNAIL:
• has a hard shell for protection;
• has a 'muddy-coloured' shell for camouflage;
• has a sticky foot for climbing on plants;
• has a rough tongue to scrape food from leaves;

The SUBMERGED PLANT:
• has very short roots because there is plenty of water;
• has stems that can be very soft because they are held up by the water.

Many living organisms are adapted to live in an oak woodland

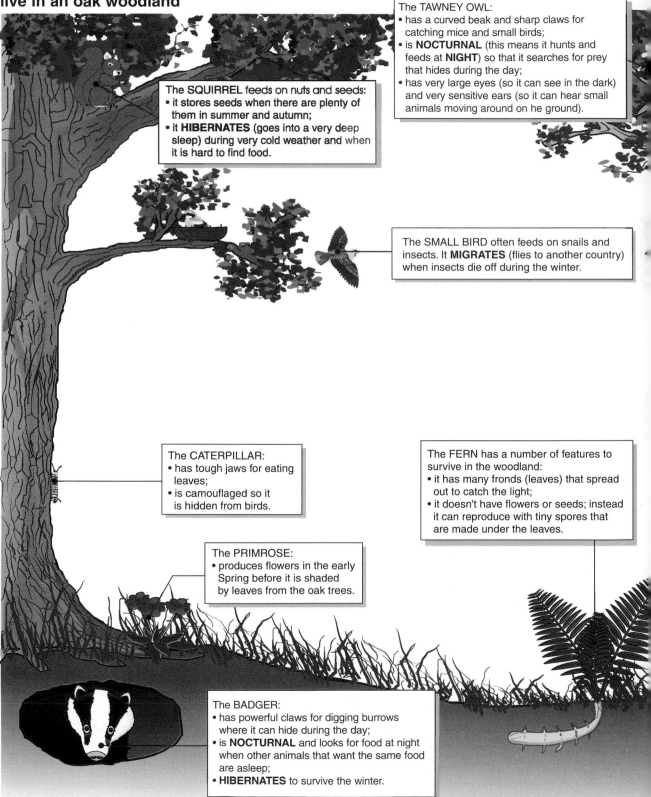

The TAWNEY OWL:
- has a curved beak and sharp claws for catching mice and small birds;
- is **NOCTURNAL** (this means it hunts and feeds at **NIGHT**) so that it searches for prey that hides during the day;
- has very large eyes (so it can see in the dark) and very sensitive ears (so it can hear small animals moving around on he ground).

The SQUIRREL feeds on nuts and seeds:
- it stores seeds when there are plenty of them in summer and autumn;
- it **HIBERNATES** (goes into a very deep sleep) during very cold weather and when it is hard to find food.

The SMALL BIRD often feeds on snails and insects. It **MIGRATES** (flies to another country) when insects die off during the winter.

The CATERPILLAR:
- has tough jaws for eating leaves;
- is camouflaged so it is hidden from birds.

The FERN has a number of features to survive in the woodland:
- it has many fronds (leaves) that spread out to catch the light;
- it doesn't have flowers or seeds; instead it can reproduce with tiny spores that are made under the leaves.

The PRIMROSE:
- produces flowers in the early Spring before it is shaded by leaves from the oak trees.

The BADGER:
- has powerful claws for digging burrows where it can hide during the day;
- is **NOCTURNAL** and looks for food at night when other animals that want the same food are asleep;
- **HIBERNATES** to survive the winter.

The OAK tree is the most important organism in this type of wood because:
• it provides food, shelter and nestling sites for other living organisms;
• it controls which other plants can grow because it takes most of the light, water and carbon dioxide in the woodland.

The WOODPECKER has many features that suit it to life in woodland:
• a tough beak to make holes in trees;
• a long tongue to reach insects deep in the holes;
• a stiff tail to hold the bird against the tree.

The BANDED SNAIL has:
• a hard shell for protection;
• a coloured shell for camouflage;
• a rough tongue to feed by scraping on leaves.

The MOUSE has:
• chisel-sharp teeth for eating seeds;
• large eyes for good night vision.

The TOADSTOOL is a fungus, so:
• it does not need light because it does not feed by photosynthesis;
• it feeds by breaking down dead plants and absorbing the food from the ground.

Exercise 10.1: Adaptation

1. Look at the 'Life in a freshwater pond' picture on pages 71-72 and give answers to the following questions.

    (a) Why is the heron a good hunter of fish?

    (b) How does a frog avoid being eaten by a heron?

    (c) Give two ways in which a stickleback fish is suited to life underwater.

    (d) What feature does a ramshorn snail have that prevents it from being washed away?

    (e) Why do small birds that eat insects migrate south for the winter? Name two such birds.

2. How is a salmon adapted to swim long distances?

3. Name two animals that hibernate. Suggest reasons why they do so.

4. What special features has an owl developed that allow it to feed successfully at night?

Extension question

5. Use a book or an Internet website to find out about how birds know which way to fly when they migrate, and then write a short paragraph describing the process.

Chapter 11
Feeding relationships

Starting point

- All living organisms need a supply of food to carry out their life processes.
- Plants use light energy and chemicals from their surroundings to make their own food.
- Animals cannot make their own food but they get their energy and raw materials from the food they eat.

Animals, and that includes humans, depend on plants for survival. There may be many different animals and plants in one habitat (see page 72, for example), but they are all linked together by food. An example of the way living organisms are linked together by food is shown below.

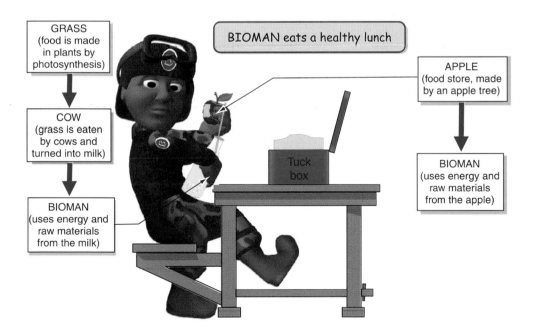

Feeding links are called food chains

These links between different organisms make up a food chain. A food chain shows how energy and raw materials are passed from one organism to another by feeding.

There are certain **rules** about food chains.

- They always start with a green plant because only green plants can make their own food. Plants make their own food by photosynthesis, so they are called **producers**.
- Animals eat or consume food, so they are called **consumers**.
- The arrows in a food chain mean 'food for'. These arrows always point in the direction in which the energy and raw materials are moving as the organisms feed.

> BIOMAN SAYS: Food chains always begin with plants. Don't forget that dead leaves, fallen branches and rotting fruit **all** came from plants.

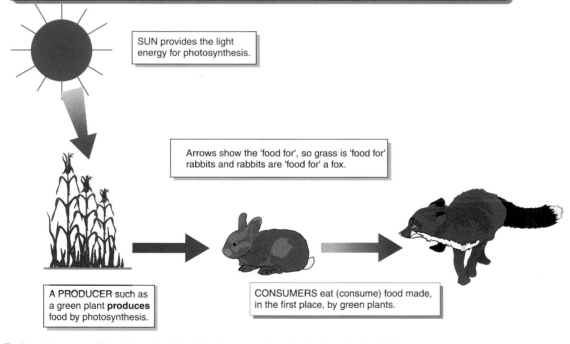

SUN provides the light energy for photosynthesis.

Arrows show the 'food for', so grass is 'food for' rabbits and rabbits are 'food for' a fox.

A PRODUCER such as a green plant **produces** food by photosynthesis.

CONSUMERS eat (consume) food made, in the first place, by green plants.

Rather than spending time drawing the plants and animals in a food chain, you can write it quite simply in words, as you can see below.

Grass ⟶ Rabbit ⟶ Fox

There are different types of consumers

Because animals cannot make their own food they must obtain their food by eating other organisms. Animals are very well adapted to the type of food they eat. Some animals (like the squirrel on page 72) are called **herbivores** because they eat plants (herba = plant or grass in Latin). Other animals, like the owl on page 73, are called **carnivores** because they eat meat (caro, carnis = meat in Latin). Some animals get the best of both worlds; they eat plants and meat. These animals are called **omnivores** (omnis = all in Latin). A badger is an omnivore, and so are humans, unless they are vegetarian of course!

Predators and prey

Animals that eat other animals are called **predators**, and the animals that they catch are called **prey**. The numbers of predators and their prey depend on each other. For example, if there are a lot of foxes (predators) in one habitat, then the rabbit (prey) numbers will quickly fall. If the number of rabbits falls, then there may not be enough food for all of the foxes. Some of the foxes will die unless they move to a place where there is more food, or they have to learn to eat other things. In Britain, many foxes have moved into cities where they have learned to feed on food thrown away by humans. The same thing can happen with insects. Greenfly can breed very quickly if the weather is warm and moist and there can be millions of them in one garden, much to the horror of the gardeners! However, a plague of greenfly is a heavenly situation for the animals that love to eat them, such as ladybirds. The ladybird numbers increase, and because there are so many of them the number of greenfly falls again. There is a cycle between the numbers of predators and their prey.

All change!

If one part of a food chain is altered, then other parts will change as well. One example of this is shown in the diagram below:

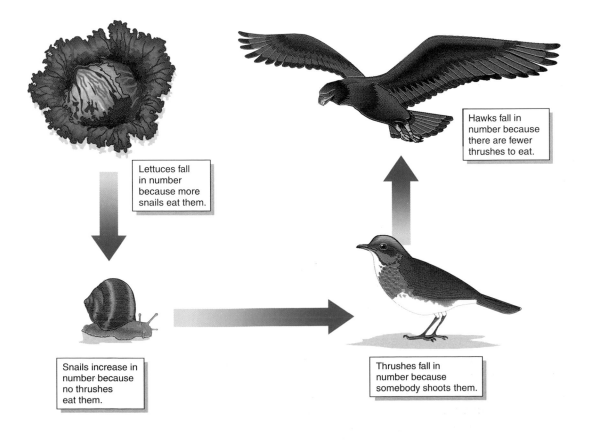

Lettuces fall in number because more snails eat them.

Hawks fall in number because there are fewer thrushes to eat.

Snails increase in number because no thrushes eat them.

Thrushes fall in number because somebody shoots them.

Exercise 11.1: Food chains

1. Look at the diagram of the oak woodland on pages 72-73.

   (a) Find an example of a herbivore, a carnivore and an omnivore from this habitat.

   (b) Identify and note down one food chain from this habitat. You will need to identify each animal and note what it feeds on. When writing down your food chain, don't forget to start with a green plant!

   (c) Give two differences that you might expect to see in an oak woodland in winter.

2. Look at the diagram of the freshwater pond on pages 70-71. Identify and note down one food chain from this habitat.

3. Think about the food that the following creatures eat. Divide them into herbivores and carnivores.

   Rabbit, lion, fox, thrush, slug, cow, horse, hyena, bat, oyster catcher, goose, heron, frog, ramshorn snail.

4. Name two animals that are omnivores.

Extension question

5. Look at this graph. It shows how the numbers of prey (snails) and predators (thrushes) change over three years.

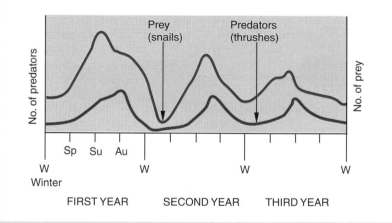

   (a) Why are there more thrushes when there are more snails?

   (b) More snails die when the winter is very cold. Which year had the coldest winter? Explain how you got this answer.

Chapter 12
Micro-organisms

- Humans need a supply of healthy food.

- Humans need to carry out their life processes efficiently if they are to stay fit and well.

Micro-organisms are living organisms that are too small to be seen without help. Scientists have discovered many different types of micro-organism (or **microbe**) by using an instrument called a **microscope**. A good microscope can **magnify** a microbe, to make it look bigger, as well as making its structure look clearer. The pictures below show three kinds of microbe, as seen through a very powerful microscope called an electron micrograph. You need to use one of these because microbes are so small that you can't see them with the naked eye, or even through a normal microscope!

Each **bacterium** is a single living organism. Millions can fit on a pinhead and they can breed very quickly in the warm, moist conditions of the body.

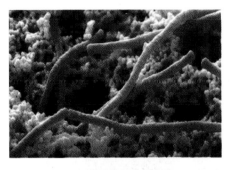

Bacteria called Lactobacillus bulgaricus taken from live yogurt. These bacteria produce lactic acid which is useful in the preservation and flavour cheese and yogurt for example.

Viruses cannot carry out life processes on their own. They are even smaller than bacteria and can only breed inside another living organism.

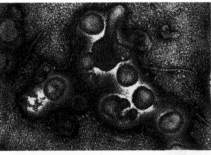

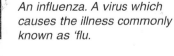

An influenza. A virus which causes the illness commonly known as 'flu.

Some organisms are made of a **single living cell** and can live in our blood and cause disease.

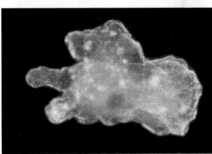

A single celled protozoan called an amoeba proteus. This one is walking!

Why do we study microbes?

Humans are very interested in microbes because some of them cause disease. These microbes live in the environment but can invade our bodies. They can get into the body in a number of different ways, as shown in the diagram below:

HOW MICROBES CAN ENTER THE BODY

Eating infected food (e.g. SALMONELLA FOOD POISONING).

Breathing in microbes from the air - possibly put there by someone sneezing (e.g. with a cold).

achoo!

Through a cut or a sore microbes can get past the skin (e.g. TETANUS).

Drinking infected water (e.g. CHOLERA).

Touching a towel already used by an infected person (e.g. CHICKEN POX).

Microbes cause disease when they interfere with the way the body works. A doctor can help the body to fight disease, for example **antiseptic creams** can kill microbes on the skin and **antibiotics** can kill bacteria that have invaded the body.

Microbes also cause problems for humans because they can make food go **mouldy**. When food is mouldy it should not be eaten because it can cause disease and can make you very ill. Mouldy food has to be thrown away, so it is wasted. Humans spend a lot of money trying to stop food going mouldy, often by improving the way it is **packaged** (in sealed tins, for example) or the way it is **stored** (in a refrigerator, for example).

Microbes can be useful

Not all microbes cause harm. Some of them are very useful, and help humans in a number of ways.

- Some are used **in food production**, for example in making cheese, bread and beer. Bacteria alter the fats in milk to give cheese its taste and smell. Yeast gets energy from sugar, and makes carbon dioxide and alcohol as side-products. The carbon dioxide makes the bread rise and the beer fizzy!

- Some help in the **breakdown of wastes,** for example in rotting down dead organisms in the soil to produce minerals for plants, and removing wastes from sewage, so we have safe drinking water.

Some of the uses of microbes are shown in the diagram below:

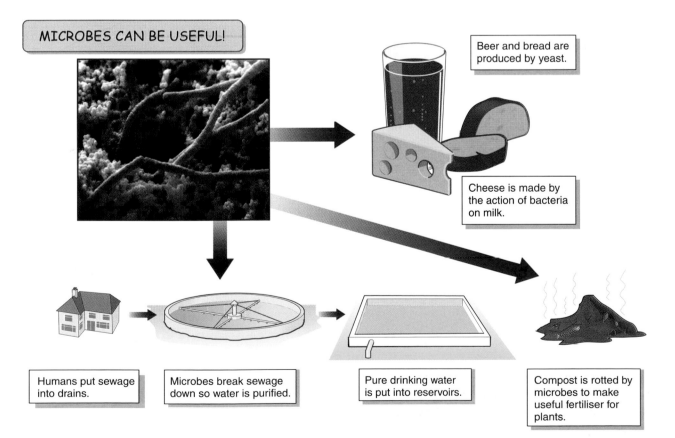

MICROBES CAN BE USEFUL!

Beer and bread are produced by yeast.

Cheese is made by the action of bacteria on milk.

Humans put sewage into drains.

Microbes break sewage down so water is purified.

Pure drinking water is put into reservoirs.

Compost is rotted by microbes to make useful fertiliser for plants.

Exercise 12.1: Microbes

1. Give the name of three groups of microbes.

2. Find out one disease caused by a bacterium and one caused by a virus.

3. Give three examples of how microbes can be useful to humans.

Extension question

4. Humans try to stop food going mouldy. Scientists tried several treatments to preserve food. They started each experiment with 100 grams of food, and changed the conditions around the food. They measured how much food was left after 48 hours. Here are their results.

Treatment	Left in normal air	Kept in fridge	Sealed away from air	Kept in dry air	Left on a radiator
Remaining food (grams)	60	98	97	98	30

(a) Why do you think most food went mouldy on the radiator?

(b) Which result shows you that oxygen is needed for food to go mouldy?

(c) Which result shows you that water is needed for food to go mouldy?

(d) What would be the best conditions to keep food from going mouldy?

Materials and their properties

We now turn to the next section and hand you over to your new guide, Material Girl who will help you to understand how different materials have different properties that enble them to do the particular jobs they do so successfully.

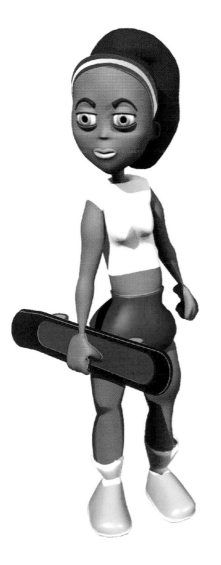

Chapter 13
Investigations in science

As we begin our next section, it is worth pausing and taking some time to learn about the rules needed to carry out scientific investigations or experiments. This section will show you:

- why scientists carry out experiments;
- what we mean by a variable;
- what we mean by a fair test;
- how we measure variables;
- how we can record and display our results;
- how we can spot a pattern in our results; and
- how we draw a conclusion from our results.

What is an experiment?

Every day we make hundreds of observations; for example 'it's raining again', 'that car is moving faster than the other one', 'that tree looks bigger today' or 'some of the pet mice are bigger than the others'. When we think like a scientist we might try to give some sort of *explanation* for what we observe. We might think that some mice are bigger than others because of what they eat. An **experiment** is a way of collecting information to check out our explanations. Before a scientist begins an experiment, he or she will have a definite **purpose** or **aim**. The aim of an experiment is a way of stating carefully what you are trying to find out.

For example:

The aim of an experiment

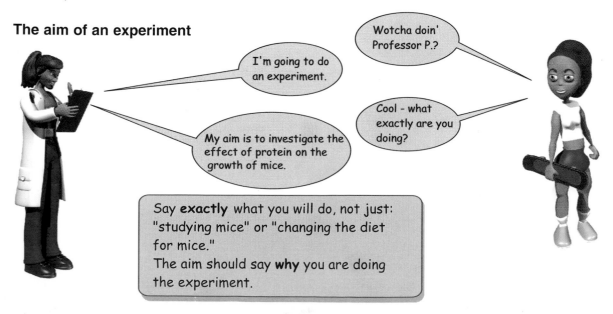

I'm going to do an experiment.

Wotcha doin' Professor P.?

My aim is to investigate the effect of protein on the growth of mice.

Cool - what exactly are you doing?

Say **exactly** what you will do, not just: "studying mice" or "changing the diet for mice."
The aim should say **why** you are doing the experiment.

What about variables?

An experiment has the aim of investigating the effect of one factor (protein in the diet, for example) on another factor (weight, for example). These factors can have different values, and so are called **variables**. In our experiment we can change the **values** of these variables, so we might give one group of mice more protein than we give another group. Anything that we can measure is a variable.

The experiment must be a fair test

An experiment will not be a **fair test** if you change more than one variable at a time.

In a fair test only one variable is changed at a time

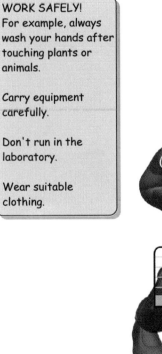

WORK SAFELY!
For example, always wash your hands after touching plants or animals.

Carry equipment carefully.

Don't run in the laboratory.

Wear suitable clothing.

FIRST: Identify the variables. Variables are factors that might affect the results.

SECOND: Choose which variable you will change. This is called the INPUT VARIABLE.

THIRD: Choose the variable that you think will be affected by changing the input variable. This is called the OUTCOME VARIABLE.

FOURTH: Decide what equipment you will need to measure any changes. Then go ahead and carry out your experiment!

IMPORTANT! To make this a FAIR TEST **only change one variable at a time**. For example, the weight of mice might be affected by:
● how old they are;
● how much water they drink;
● the other foods they eat;
● how big their cage is.
If you want to investigate how protein affects the weight of mice, all these other variables **must stay the same**.

How we measure variables

During an experiment a scientist will change one variable; this is called the **input variable**. The scientist will want to find out if the change in this variable causes a change in another variable. This second variable is called the **outcome variable**. To make sure that the experiment is a fair test the scientist will also want to check that none of the other possible variables is changing. Scientists like you need special equipment to measure any changes in these variables. Some of these pieces of equipment, and what you would use them for, have already been described in this book. This table will give you a quick reminder:

Table 1: Measuring equipment for use in Science

Equipment	What it measures	Units (Symbol)
Forcemeter	Force	Newtons (N)
Balance	Weight	Grams (g)
Stopwatch	Time	Seconds (s)
Measuring cylinder	Volume	Millilitres (ml) and litres (l)
Ruler/tape measure	Length	Millimetres (mm) and metres (m)
Thermometer	Temperature	Degrees Celsius (°C)

Making a record of our results

Results (or **observations**) are a record of the measurements you have taken during an experiment. There are certain rules about the way you should show these results. They should be recorded in a table, like the one shown on the next page.

Making a table of results

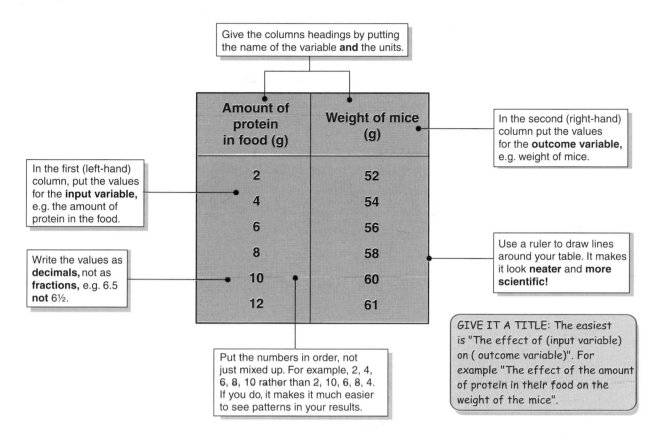

Give the columns headings by putting the name of the variable **and** the units.

Amount of protein in food (g)	Weight of mice (g)
2	52
4	54
6	56
8	58
10	60
12	61

In the first (left-hand) column, put the values for the **input variable,** e.g. the amount of protein in the food.

Write the values as **decimals,** not as **fractions,** e.g. 6.5 **not** 6½.

In the second (right-hand) column put the values for the **outcome variable,** e.g. weight of mice.

Use a ruler to draw lines around your table. It makes it look **neater** and **more scientific!**

Put the numbers in order, not just mixed up. For example, 2, 4, 6, 8, 10 rather than 2, 10, 6, 8, 4. If you do, it makes it much easier to see patterns in your results.

GIVE IT A TITLE: The easiest is "The effect of (input variable) on (outcome variable)". For example "The effect of the amount of protein in their food on the weight of the mice".

When you look at your results, you may see a certain pattern. It might seem that the more protein a mouse gets in its diet, for example, the faster it grows.

- Your results will be more reliable if you carry out each test more than once, and then take an **average** of the results. Why? (I hear you ask.) Just think about it; if you happen to get the greediest mouse this side of Timbuctoo, your results are going to be somewhat unusual. Whereas if you do the experiment on ten mice and take the average, it is a fair test.

- If one or two of the results don't fit the pattern, the first thing to do is check your measurement. If your measurement was accurate, and you have the time, you can **repeat** the test to check the 'odd' result.

Displaying your results

Sometimes you can see a pattern in your results from the table you have made. It isn't always easy to spot a pattern directly from a table, and it may be better to look at them in another way. **Charts** and **graphs** display your results like pictures and they can make it very easy to see patterns, but only if they are drawn in the correct way. There are rules for drawing graphs and charts, just as there are rules for putting results into tables.

- First of all, look at the variables you measured. If both of the variables had numbers as their values, you should draw (sometimes we say 'plot') a **line graph**. If one of the variables isn't measured in numbers, you should choose a **bar chart**.

- You should always put the **input variable** on the **horizontal** axis and the **outcome variable** on the **vertical** axis. If you don't do this, you can easily mix up the patterns between the two variables.

This is how to draw a bar chart

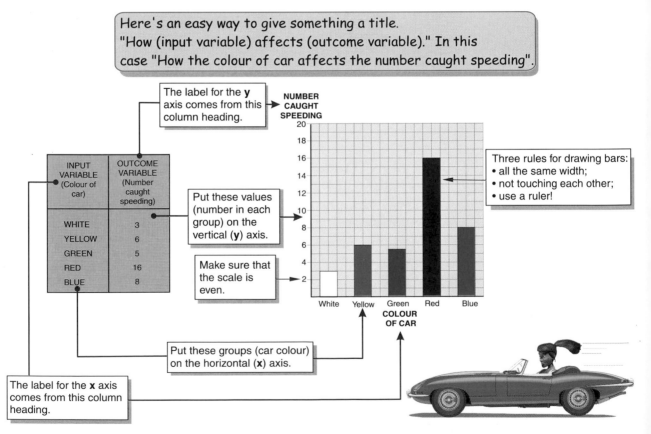

Here's an easy way to give something a title.
"How (input variable) affects (outcome variable)." In this case "How the colour of car affects the number caught speeding".

The label for the **y** axis comes from this column heading.

INPUT VARIABLE (Colour of car)	OUTCOME VARIABLE (Number caught speeding)
WHITE	3
YELLOW	6
GREEN	5
RED	16
BLUE	8

Put these values (number in each group) on the vertical (**y**) axis.

Make sure that the scale is even.

Three rules for drawing bars:
- all the same width;
- not touching each other;
- use a ruler!

Put these groups (car colour) on the horizontal (**x**) axis.

The label for the **x** axis comes from this column heading.

How to draw a line graph

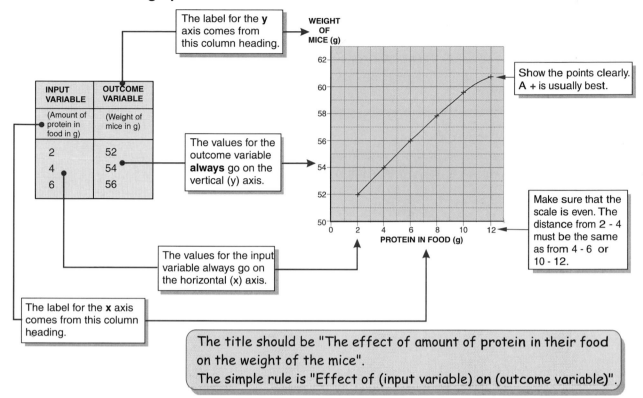

The label for the **y** axis comes from this column heading.

Show the points clearly. A + is usually best.

The values for the outcome variable **always** go on the vertical (y) axis.

Make sure that the scale is even. The distance from 2 - 4 must be the same as from 4 - 6 or 10 - 12.

The values for the input variable always go on the horizontal (x) axis.

The label for the **x** axis comes from this column heading.

The title should be "The effect of amount of protein in their food on the weight of the mice".
The simple rule is "Effect of (input variable) on (outcome variable)".

INPUT VARIABLE	OUTCOME VARIABLE
(Amount of protein in food in g)	(Weight of mice in g)
2	52
4	54
6	56

Using graphs

A graph can let you see a pattern between two variables. For example, as protein in their diet increases, so does the weight of mice. The graph can also let you make **predictions** if it shows an obvious pattern. So, you might be able to predict how much a mouse would weigh if it was fed on a diet containing a certain amount of protein.

Just before we look at how to do this using a graph, it is worth making an important point about predictions. It is in fact very useful indeed to make some of your own predictions even **before** you get started on your experiment. If you do this, it can help you to plan much better experiments. If we take the example of looking at the effect protein has on the weight of the mice eating it, we can make a pretty good guess (a prediction) that the more we feed them, the heavier they are likely to become. We can also start to plan what apparatus we will need and so on.

Right, now you know this you can have a look on the next page to see how we can use graphs to help make predictions.

Using a graph to make a prediction

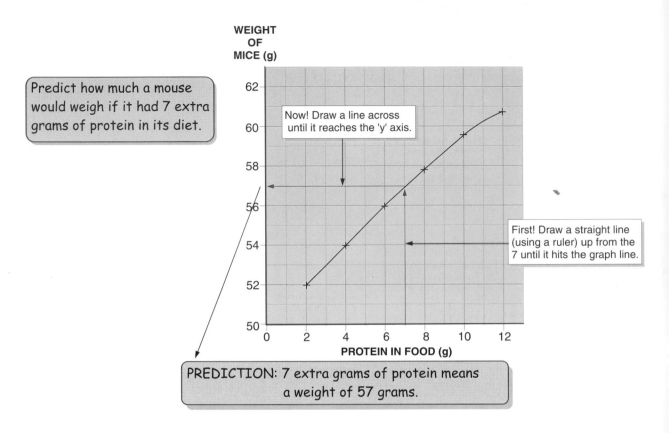

> Predict how much a mouse would weigh if it had 7 extra grams of protein in its diet.

Now! Draw a line across until it reaches the 'y' axis.

First! Draw a straight line (using a ruler) up from the 7 until it hits the graph line.

PREDICTION: 7 extra grams of protein means a weight of 57 grams.

Making conclusions

Once you have collected all of your results into a table, and perhaps drawn a graph or chart, you need to sum up what you have found out. This summing up is called a **conclusion**, and here are some tips:

- **Your conclusion should be related to the aim of your experiment.**
  If your aim was to investigate the effect of light intensity on plant growth and you saw a clear pattern, then your conclusion might be that 'the higher the light intensity, the taller the plant'.

- **Try to write your conclusion simply** (one sentence is often enough) but make sure it explains how the input variable affects the outcome variable for your experiment.

- **Don't just describe your results.**
  For example, in the experiment on mouse growth the statement 'a lot of protein in the diet makes a mouse heavy' is really only giving one of your results. A much better conclusion would be 'the greater the amount of protein in the diet, the heavier the mouse becomes'.

Made to measure

As we now know, scientists often need to measure things during the course of their experiments. Some examples of measuring devices are shown in the next few diagrams.

Measuring length using a ruler

A ruler can be made of plastic. The plastic can be made into the correct shape, and it can be marked to show the measurements on the ruler. This diagram reminds you how to use a ruler.

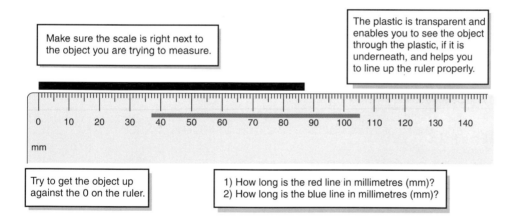

> Make sure the scale is right next to the object you are trying to measure.

> The plastic is transparent and enables you to see the object through the plastic, if it is underneath, and helps you to line up the ruler properly.

> Try to get the object up against the 0 on the ruler.

> 1) How long is the red line in millimetres (mm)?
> 2) How long is the blue line in millimetres (mm)?

Measuring volume using a beaker or a measuring cylinder

Beakers and **measuring cylinders** can be made out of plastic. Many of these pieces of equipment are made of glass, but glass is quite likely to break. Scientists now often use plastic because it is usually safer. However, plastic beakers can't be used to boil liquids because they would melt and become distorted and useless.

The diagram on the next page shows you how to use a measuring cylinder and a beaker.

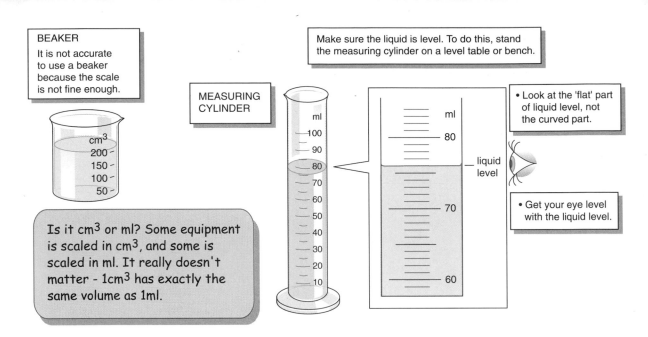

BEAKER
It is not accurate to use a beaker because the scale is not fine enough.

Make sure the liquid is level. To do this, stand the measuring cylinder on a level table or bench.

MEASURING CYLINDER

• Look at the 'flat' part of liquid level, not the curved part.

liquid level

• Get your eye level with the liquid level.

Is it cm^3 or ml? Some equipment is scaled in cm^3, and some is scaled in ml. It really doesn't matter - 1cm^3 has exactly the same volume as 1ml.

Measuring other things

There are other things that scientists want to measure. These include temperature, force and mass. Measuring temperature is described on page 135 and measuring force is described on page 178.

Measuring mass using a balance

Mass is the name scientists give to the amount of a substance. You can use a **balance** (also called a **weighing machine**) to measure the mass of something. It is very important to remember that if you are weighing liquid which is in a container, you must subtract the weight of the container. You can do this as follows:

Step 1   Weigh the empty beaker. Note down its mass.

Step 2   Add the liquid and weigh the beaker again. Note down this mass.

Step 3   Subtract the mass of the empty beaker (step 1) from the mass of the beaker containing liquid (step 2).

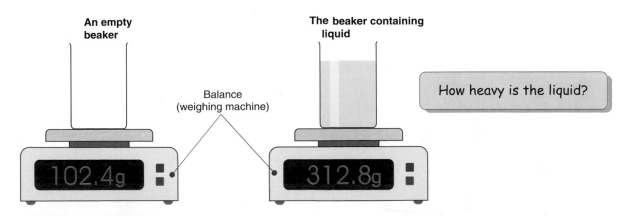

An empty beaker

The beaker containing liquid

Balance (weighing machine)

How heavy is the liquid?

102.4g

312.8g

Exercise 13.1: Made to measure

1. Give two reasons why glass and plastic are useful materials.

2. Give one reason why glass is more useful than plastic when making measuring equipment.

3. Give one reason why plastic is more useful than glass when making measuring equipment.

Extension questions

4. Look at these diagrams. A scientist has measured the mass and the volume of some water and some alcohol. What can you tell from the measurements?

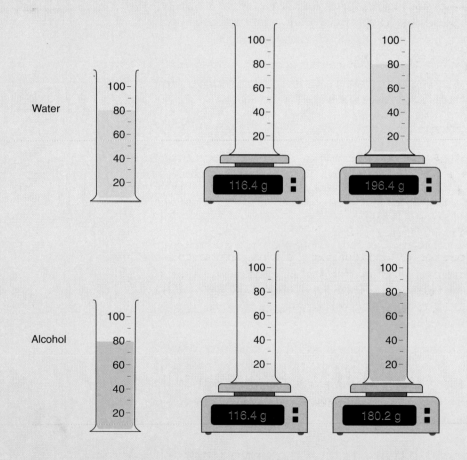

5. Minnie is going on a trip, and she wants to take some water. She has a water container that weighs 120 grams. She doesn't want to carry more than 260 grams altogether. What is the maximum weight of water she should take with her?

Chapter 14
Materials and their properties

In the **life and living processes** section we met one group of scientists, called biologists. Biologists, as we now know, are interested in the study of living things.

Another group of scientists study the **properties of material substances**, and how they can be changed from one thing to another. Substances can change in two ways. They can undergo chemical changes which are studied by a group of scientists called **chemists**; and they also undergo physical changes, studied by another group of scientists called **physicists**.

We often do things in our daily lives that make us appear to be like chemists and physicists. As we go through this section, just think about how many times you have changed material substances from one thing to another.

Here are some examples of material changes. You can see why this whole subject is fascinating and indeed how important it is that we understand the way these changes happen.

Life: Living things are constantly changing one substance to another. Remember how plants change carbon dioxide and water into sugar and oxygen? So life is all about chemistry.

Cooking: Think how a baker changes flour, sugar, yeast and water into bread, or how a cake maker beats an egg white with sugar to make a meringue.

Engineering: Engineers use their knowledge of different substances when they decide what materials to use for making things. It would be no good making a bridge out of rubber!

Making clothes: A clothing designer needs to know exactly what different substances will do when they are worn. For example, a jacket will need to be made from a material that is light but warm and the soles of trainers will need to be made from a material that gives good grip, doesn't wear out very quickly and doesn't let water in.

Materials are substances for making things

Everything in the world is made from substances. The substances that make up all the objects in the world are called materials. Different materials have different properties that make them suitable for the job they do. Scientists try to understand the properties of different materials and then use or make the material they need for a particular job.

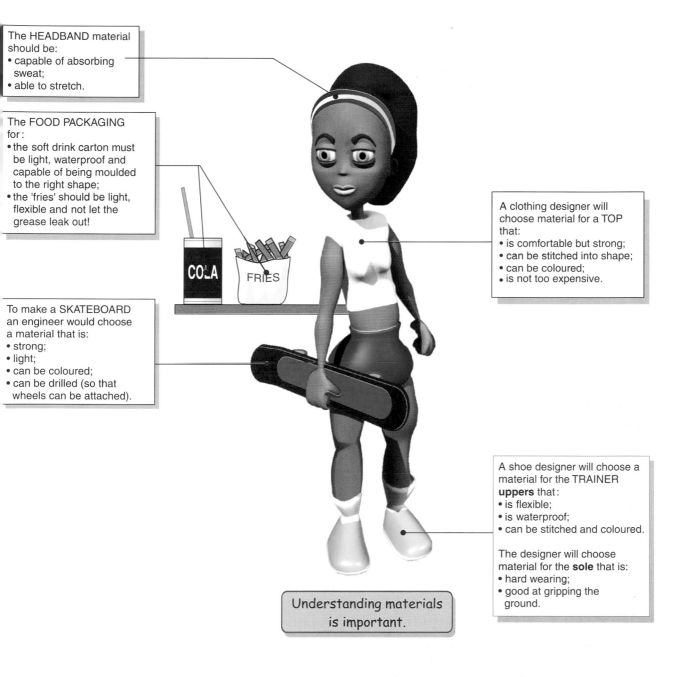

The HEADBAND material should be:
• capable of absorbing sweat;
• able to stretch.

The FOOD PACKAGING for:
• the soft drink carton must be light, waterproof and capable of being moulded to the right shape;
• the 'fries' should be light, flexible and not let the grease leak out!

To make a SKATEBOARD an engineer would choose a material that is:
• strong;
• light;
• can be coloured;
• can be drilled (so that wheels can be attached).

A clothing designer will choose material for a TOP that:
• is comfortable but strong;
• can be stitched into shape;
• can be coloured;
• is not too expensive.

A shoe designer will choose a material for the TRAINER **uppers** that:
• is flexible;
• is waterproof;
• can be stitched and coloured.

The designer will choose material for the **sole** that is:
• hard wearing;
• good at gripping the ground.

COLA

FRIES

Understanding materials is important.

Suited to the job: what are the important properties of materials?

If we want to choose a material for a particular job, we have to ask some basic questions before we can decide which one to use.

- Does it have the right **physical properties**? Physical properties mean things like hardness, strength, how easily it melts and whether or not you can see through it.

- Does it have the right **chemical properties**? Chemical properties are to do with how the material reacts with other materials. We would want to know whether it burns easily or whether it goes rusty in water.

- How much does it **cost**? For some jobs it is not a good idea to choose a material that has the properties you want if it costs an absolute fortune.

Choosing the right material for a job means getting the right balance between physical properties, chemical properties and cost.

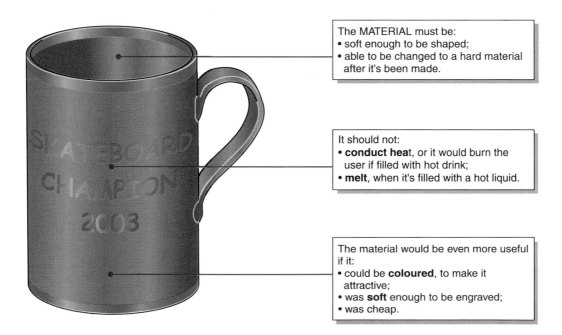

The MATERIAL must be:
- soft enough to be shaped;
- able to be changed to a hard material after it's been made.

It should not:
- **conduct heat**, or it would burn the user if filled with hot drink;
- **melt**, when it's filled with a hot liquid.

The material would be even more useful if it:
- could be **coloured**, to make it attractive;
- was **soft** enough to be engraved;
- was cheap.

Exercise 14.1: Choosing materials

1. (a) A manufacturer wants to make some rubber riding boots. Give two important physical properties that he should be looking for in deciding which material to use.

   (b) The same manufacturer also wants to make some horse shoes. Which physical properties should he be looking for in deciding which material to use.

2. Which important chemical properties should a manufacturer be looking for when making the following?

   (a) A kettle

   (b) A mug

   (c) A saucepan handle

   Explain why you made your choices for each item.

Extension questions

3. Study this table which describes the properties of some materials and then answer the questions below.

Material	Description	Strength	Flexibility	Cost
Aluminium	A silvery metal which doesn't rust.	Medium	Medium	Low
Steel (Steel is made from iron and other metals mixed together.)	A grey material which rusts easily unless protected.	High	Low	Low
Wood	A brown material which rots unless protected.	Medium	Medium	Low
Polythene	A plastic which can be coloured.	Low	High	Low
Kevlar	A plastic which can be given any colour.	High	Low	High

   Which would be the best material for making the following objects? Explain how you made your choice.

   (a) The body of a car

   (b) A garden fence

   (c) Supermarket shopping bags

   (d) A railway bridge

4. From what you know about properties, explain why a household plate is made of china but a picnic plate is made of plastic.

Classifying materials

Material Girl says:

- everything in the world is made from materials;
- materials all have different properties and that means that they are good at performing different jobs.

Classifying materials

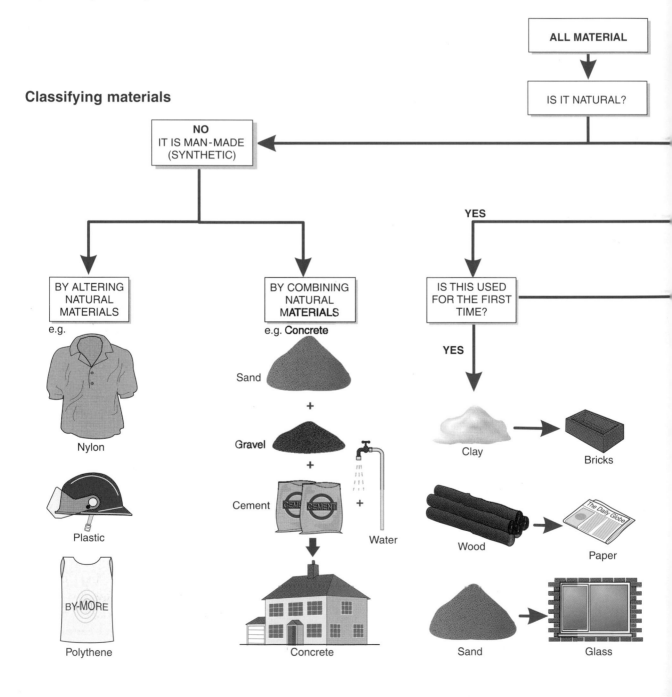

Where do materials come from?

If you want to choose a material for a certain job, you need to know its properties. It is also useful, and interesting, to know where the material came from. When you classify **living** things you split them into groups. Well, you can classify materials into groups too! Remember how scientists like to bring order into their world?

There are several questions that you could ask as you set out on your mission to classify materials into groups.

- Is the material natural or man-made?
- Has the material been changed, by heating for example?
- Is the material made by combining other materials?

If you use questions like this you could make a key for materials, like the one below.

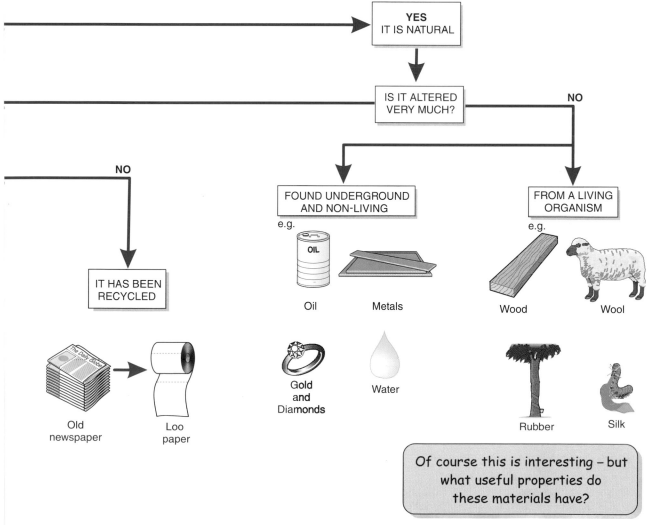

Of course this is interesting – but what useful properties do these materials have?

Rigidity: Rigid materials are very **stiff**. They can therefore be useful in building houses and making bridges. Most rigid materials are also very strong.

Aluminium ladder

Wooden hammer handle

Transparency: We can see through a transparent material. This is useful if we need to know what is on the other side of an object.

Glass window

Plastic visor on motorcycle helmet

Opacity: Opaque materials are the opposite of transparent ones (i.e. light cannot pass through them). This is useful if we want to hide an object, or protect it from light.

Fabric / plastic shower curtain

Plastic medicine bottle

Absorbency: Absorbent materials can soak up liquids. They are useful when we want to dry something that has got wet, or to prevent a liquid spreading.

Paper nappies

Textile towel

Being waterproof: A waterproof material doesn't let water pass through it because it repels the water. Waterproof materials are used to protect other objects from water – you for example!

Nylon oversuit

Ceramic sink

Glass and plastic are two important materials. Both of these materials have properties that are very useful to us. Both glass and some plastics:

- are **transparent** which means that we can see through them;
- can be **moulded** into different shapes; and
- can be **marked** with scratches and coloured paints.

Glass and plastic are transparent which means they let light pass through.

Glass and plastic do not dissolve in water, and this includes rainwater.

No skateboarding today!

Glass does not scratch as easily as plastic.

If the glass breaks, the pieces are very **sharp.**

These properties mean that glass and some plastics are especially useful to scientists. They can be used to make scientific equipment, including equipment that can be used for measuring things. We saw some of these in the 'Made to measure' section of this book (page 91).

Exercise 15.1: Metals and magnets

1. The Government has made very strict laws about getting rid of old cars. Materials from old cars must be recycled as much as possible.

   (a) Look at this diagram, then complete the table by matching the parts of the car to the materials used:

Material	Part of car
Steel	
Alloy (containing iron)	
Plastic	
Rubber	
Glass	

   (b) Make a list of three parts of a car that could be collected with a magnet. Make another list of three parts of a car that could not be collected with a magnet.

2. Use words from this list to complete the paragraph about metals.

MAGNETIC	SHINY	FLEXIBLE
STEEL	HARD	WATER
ELECTRICITY	MERCURY	IRON

Metals are usually .... which is useful if they are going to be polished and ....

Most metals conduct heat and .... A few metals are .... which means that

they can be separated from other metals. One metal is very different from the others. This metal, called

......................................, is actually a liquid at room temperature. Some metals, such as ....,

are produced by mixing other metals together.

Chapter 16
Solids, liquids and gases

- Everything on the Earth is made of materials.
- Different materials have different properties.

All of the materials fall into one of three groups: solids, liquids or gases. These three different groups of materials have different properties which can affect the jobs they are used for. The most important properties are explained below.

- Whether or not the material can **flow**. Gases and liquids flow, but solids do not.
- Whether or not the material can **change shape**. Solids keep the same shape, liquids change shape to fill the container they are in and gases spread out to fill any space they can reach. We can change the shape of a solid, by getting rid of some of it, or bending it.
- Whether or not the material can be squeezed to **change its volume**. The volume of a gas can be changed easily by squashing it. Liquids and solids normally don't change very much in volume, and they can expand very slightly when heated.

Properties of solids, liquids and gases.

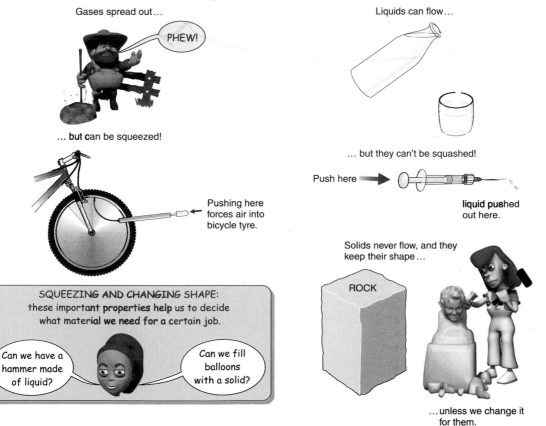

Gases spread out…

PHEW!

… but can be squeezed!

Pushing here forces air into bicycle tyre.

Liquids can flow…

… but they can't be squashed!

Push here

liquid pushed out here.

Solids never flow, and they keep their shape…

ROCK

…unless we change it for them.

SQUEEZING AND CHANGING SHAPE: these important **properties help us** to decide what material **we need** for a certain job.

Can we have a hammer made of liquid?

Can we fill balloons with a solid?

Explaining the properties

All materials are made up of tiny **particles**. The way these particles are arranged helps to explain the different properties of solids, liquids and gases.

In **gases** the particles are a long way away from each other but they all bounce around hitting each other and this keeps them apart. Gases flow easily and spread out to fill any available space. A gas is mostly empty space you can easily squeeze the particles together into a smaller space which is why it is easy to change the volume of a gas.

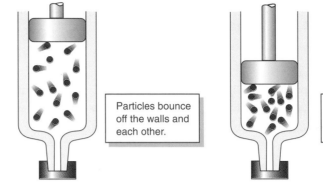

Particles bounce off the walls and each other.

Particles can be squeezed closer together.

In **liquids** the particles are very close together, but they don't hold onto each other very strongly. Although the particles in a liquid stay close together they are always moving around one another, in fact they change places all the time. This is why liquids flow so easily, and why they can take up the shape of the container they are in. There is no space between the particles, so you can't squeeze a liquid into a smaller space.

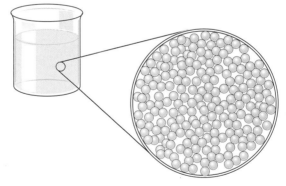

The particles in a liquid move around each other. There is no pattern.

In **solids** the particles are packed very closely together and hold onto each other so tightly that they can hardly move at all. This is why solids don't flow and why they keep their shape. Because the particles are so close together, solids can't be squashed into a smaller volume. There are two types of solid: crystals, where the particles are in a fixed pattern (as shown here), and other solids, where the particles are not arranged in quite such a tidy way.

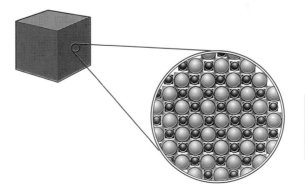

Particles in a solid are fixed in a pattern, so you can't change its shape or volume unless you chop it up!

Exercise 16.1: Solids, liquids and gases

1. Copy out and complete this table about the properties of solids, liquids and gases

	Solids	Liquids	Gases
Do they flow easily?			
Can they be compressed?			
Can they change their shape?			
Are the particles close together or far apart?			
Do the particles hold onto each other tightly or not?			

2. Match these types of material to their possible use. Choose from solid, liquid or gas.

(a) A .... can act as a roof support.

(b) A .... can be squeezed into a container.

(c) A .... can be pushed through a pipe.

(d) A .... can be used to fill up a balloon.

(e) A .... can be made into a tool.

(f) A .... can be poured from one container into another.

Air is a good insulator

Air does not allow heat to pass through it very easily. Air can be trapped to form a layer of insulation. The insulation can then prevent heat from moving into an object as well as preventing heat moving out of an object. Some examples of the use of trapped air as an insulator are shown below:

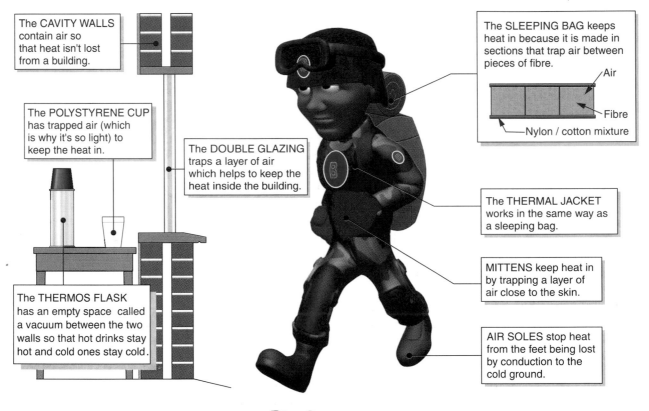

The CAVITY WALLS contain air so that heat isn't lost from a building.

The POLYSTYRENE CUP has trapped air (which is why it's so light) to keep the heat in.

The DOUBLE GLAZING traps a layer of air which helps to keep the heat inside the building.

The THERMOS FLASK has an empty space called a vacuum between the two walls so that hot drinks stay hot and cold ones stay cold.

The SLEEPING BAG keeps heat in because it is made in sections that trap air between pieces of fibre.

Air

Fibre

Nylon / cotton mixture

The THERMAL JACKET works in the same way as a sleeping bag.

MITTENS keep heat in by trapping a layer of air close to the skin.

AIR SOLES stop heat from the feet being lost by conduction to the cold ground.

Fig.3

Exercise 17.1: The conduction of heat

1. Why do a knife and fork feel colder than the table they are lying on?

2. Why does glass in a window feel cooler than the wooden window frame around it?

3. Put these materials into order of heat conduction with the best conductor first and the worst one last:

   STEEL, PLASTIC, GLASS, AIR, WOOD, CLOTH.

4. Look at figure 3, above. Can you see any other examples of insulation, apart from the air?

Extension question

5. Read through the section on solids, liquids and gases (page 109). Use the information in that section to try to explain why a metal is a better conductor of heat than air.

The passage of electricity: conductors and insulators

Don't forget

- Different materials have different properties.
- Many metals have the property of conducting electricity.

The movement of electricity

Electricity is a very useful form of energy. It can be used to power electric motors, like those that drive a train, for example. It can also be used to 'light up' a light bulb, or to provide the heat from an electric fire. Electricity needs something to travel through, to get from the place where it's made to the place where it is used. Materials that can carry electricity are called **conductors**.

Conductors and insulators

The materials that are used most frequently as conductors are metals, such as copper used in wiring, and graphite which is a form of the element called carbon. There are also other conductors but they aren't so easy to use. Water for example, is not easy to control and use, but can be a very good conductor which is why it is so dangerous to be near a source of electricity in wet conditions.

Not all materials are conductors of electricity. The materials that do not conduct electricity are called **insulators**. Non-metallic substances are usually good insulators. Plastic, rubber, glass and wood are good examples, but don't let them get wet!

Conductors and insulators work together

Insulators and conductors both have important uses, and are often found together. Household wiring and electrical appliances give us a very good example of this. We must be able to:

- conduct electricity into our houses from the mains supply out in the street;
- conduct electricity to the different rooms in the house;
- connect electrical appliances, like a TV or electric kettle, to the electricity supply;

... and these jobs all need to be done without the risk of electrocuting ourselves!

Chapter 18
Rocks and soils

Remember

- Some materials are natural and some are synthetic.
- The different properties of materials mean that humans can choose the right material for a particular job.

Rocks are found in many parts of the world, for example on beaches, buried underground and on mountainsides. They make up the crust of the Earth and because they have useful properties they have been used by humans for thousands of years. There are so many different kinds of rock that we need to divide them into groups. We can base these groups on the different **physical properties** that rocks possess.

- **Hardness:** Some rocks are harder than others which, of course, affects what jobs they can be used for.
- **Permeability:** Some rocks allow water to soak through them, but others do not. This property helps us to choose a particular rock for a certain job. You would not want a leaky chalk washbasin!
- **Appearance and texture:** Some rocks feel rough and some feel smooth. Some look the same all the way through their structure whilst others seem to be made of a mixture of several kinds of rock.

Some examples of these types of rock are shown in the diagram below:

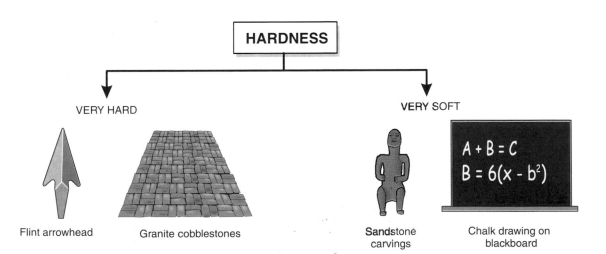

HARDNESS

VERY HARD   VERY SOFT

Flint arrowhead   Granite cobblestones   Sandstone carvings   Chalk drawing on blackboard

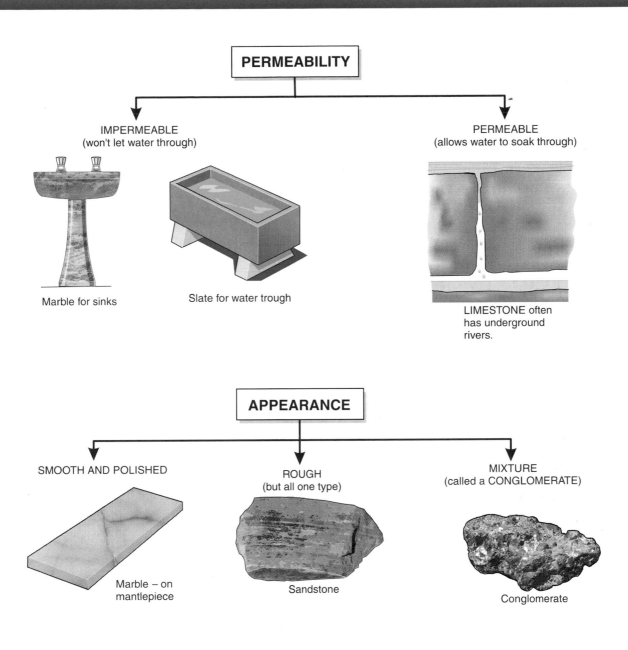

PERMEABILITY

IMPERMEABLE
(won't let water through)

Marble for sinks

Slate for water trough

PERMEABLE
(allows water to soak through)

LIMESTONE often has underground rivers.

APPEARANCE

SMOOTH AND POLISHED

Marble – on mantlepiece

ROUGH
(but all one type)

Sandstone

MIXTURE
(called a CONGLOMERATE)

Conglomerate

A fossilised Jurassic ammonite (195-140 million years old) in limestone
Fossils are rocks that have the shapes of animals, fish or plants in them. These animals and plants have been dead for millions of years.

Soil is made from rock

Think about this:

- rocks make up the crust of the Earth;
- different rocks have different physical properties, especially in terms of hardness and permeability.

Soil covers a great deal of the land, but it hasn't always been there. Soil is made from two main parts:

- small pieces of **rock** which have been made by the **weathering** of larger pieces of rock; and
- **humus** which is the decaying remains of dead animals and plants.

Soil also contains air, water, dissolved mineral salts and thousands of living organisms.

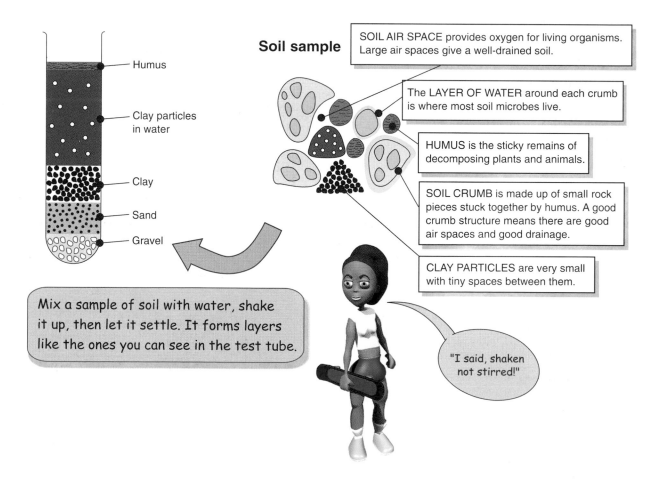

Humus

Clay particles in water

Clay

Sand

Gravel

Soil sample

SOIL AIR SPACE provides oxygen for living organisms. Large air spaces give a well-drained soil.

The LAYER OF WATER around each crumb is where most soil microbes live.

HUMUS is the sticky remains of decomposing plants and animals.

SOIL CRUMB is made up of small rock pieces stuck together by humus. A good crumb structure means there are good air spaces and good drainage.

CLAY PARTICLES are very small with tiny spaces between them.

Mix a sample of soil with water, shake it up, then let it settle. It forms layers like the ones you can see in the test tube.

"I said, shaken not stirred!"

Weathering of rock: how soil is formed

The process of breaking large rocks into smaller ones is called **weathering** and that's because most of the work is done by the weather! How this happens is shown in the diagram below. Notice that the roots of plants and the burrowing of small animals also help to form a fertile soil.

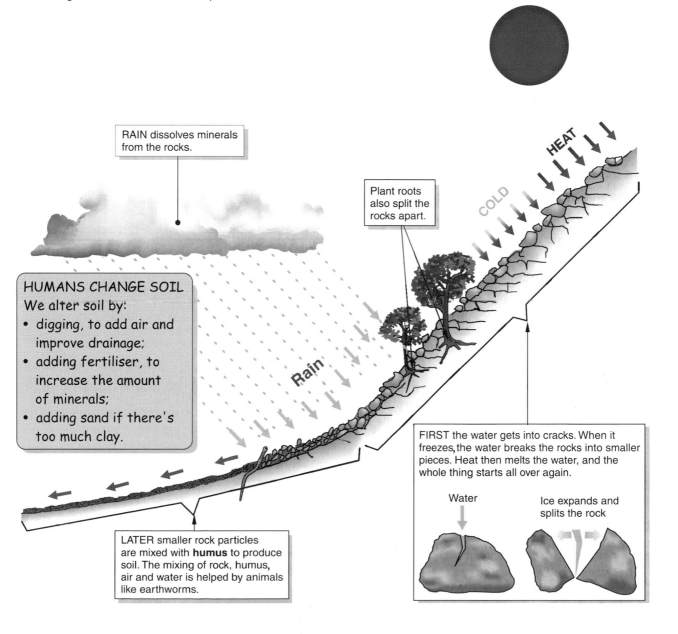

RAIN dissolves minerals from the rocks.

Plant roots also split the rocks apart.

HEAT

COLD

Rain

HUMANS CHANGE SOIL
We alter soil by:
- digging, to add air and improve drainage;
- adding fertiliser, to increase the amount of minerals;
- adding sand if there's too much clay.

FIRST the water gets into cracks. When it freezes, the water breaks the rocks into smaller pieces. Heat then melts the water, and the whole thing starts all over again.

Water

Ice expands and splits the rock

LATER smaller rock particles are mixed with **humus** to produce soil. The mixing of rock, humus, air and water is helped by animals like earthworms.

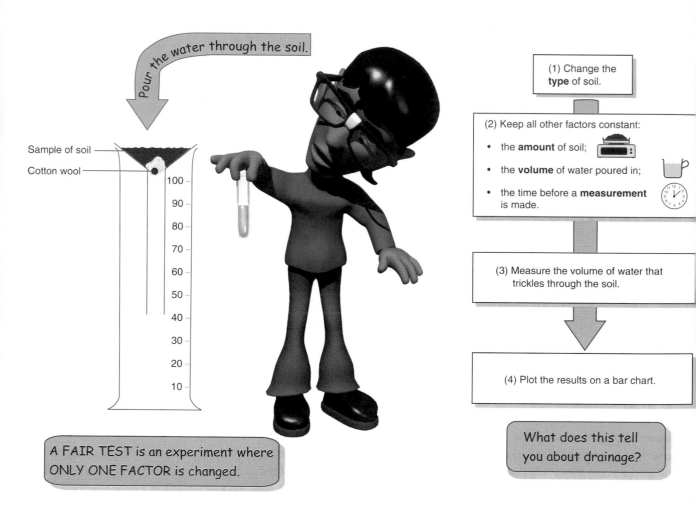

Pour the water through the soil.

Sample of soil
Cotton wool

100
90
80
70
60
50
40
30
20
10

(1) Change the **type** of soil.

(2) Keep all other factors constant:
- the **amount** of soil;
- the **volume** of water poured in;
- the time before a **measurement** is made.

(3) Measure the volume of water that trickles through the soil.

(4) Plot the results on a bar chart.

A FAIR TEST is an experiment where ONLY ONE FACTOR is changed.

What does this tell you about drainage?

Exercise 18.2: Soil

1. Name the type of soil that is best for growing crops. Explain why you made this choice.

2. Soils are very different. Copy and complete this table of soil properties.

Soil type	Sandy	Clay	Loam
Particle size			
Air spaces			
Drainage			
Amount of humus			
Amount of minerals			

Extension question

3. This apparatus can be used to collect tiny animals that live in a sample of soil.

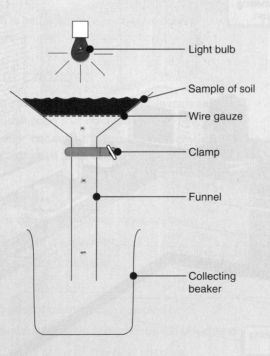

- Light bulb
- Sample of soil
- Wire gauze
- Clamp
- Funnel
- Collecting beaker

(a) Give two ways in which the lamp will affect the soil.

(b) What will the animals do if the lamp is left on?

(c) What is the name of the instrument you would use to look at the animals?

(d) A scientist wanted to use the apparatus to compare the number of animals in three different soil samples. Why was it important that he tested the same amount of each soil sample?

Exercise 19.1: Changing materials

1. Look at these diagrams. Copy the table, and complete the second column saying whether each change is a physical or a chemical change. Write a reason for your choice in the third column.

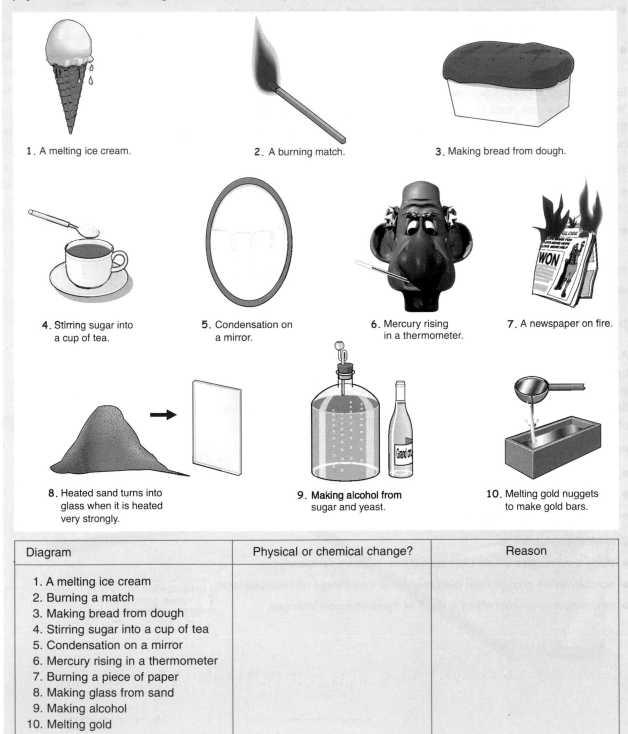

1. A melting ice cream.

2. A burning match.

3. Making bread from dough.

4. Stirring sugar into a cup of tea.

5. Condensation on a mirror.

6. Mercury rising in a thermometer.

7. A newspaper on fire.

8. Heated sand turns into glass when it is heated very strongly.

9. Making alcohol from sugar and yeast.

10. Melting gold nuggets to make gold bars.

Diagram	Physical or chemical change?	Reason
1. A melting ice cream		
2. Burning a match		
3. Making bread from dough		
4. Stirring sugar into a cup of tea		
5. Condensation on a mirror		
6. Mercury rising in a thermometer		
7. Burning a piece of paper		
8. Making glass from sand		
9. Making alcohol		
10. Melting gold		

Making solutions: mixing with water

Starting points

- Materials can be changed.
- One kind of change takes place when materials are mixed.
- Some changes produce new substances, whilst others do not.

The appearance of some materials changes when they are mixed with water. You can see this if you stir a spoonful of salt into a glass of water; the salt seems to disappear. What has happened is that the salt has dissolved in the water. The new mixture is called a **solution**, and in fact the salt hasn't disappeared at all. The particles of the salt have spread out, so that you can't see them, but they are still there.

This is an example of a **physical change** because no new materials have been produced; the materials have just changed the way they look.

Some other examples of creating solutions are shown in the diagram below:

Coffee granules dissolve in hot water to produce a solution of coffee.

GASES AND LIQUIDS ALSO DISSOLVE.
Gases, for example oxygen, can dissolve in water, which is good for fish. Some liquids can also dissolve in water. Alcohol is a good example of this.

Sugar dissolves in coffee to make a sweet, sugary solution.

An aspirin dissolves in water to make a fizzy solution.

Dilute or concentrated

A solution with a lot of dissolved material in it is **concentrated** (sometimes we say it is 'strong'), and a solution with very little dissolved material in it is **dilute** (or 'weak'). We concentrate a solution by adding more solute to it, and we can dilute a solution by adding more solvent to it. Orange squash for example, is concentrated, but we can dilute it by adding water (the solvent).

You will find out something about separating the materials in mixtures on page 156.

Exercise 19.2: Solutions

1. Match up words from the first column with the correct definitions from the second column.

Word	Definition
Dissolve	The name for a substance that dissolves in a liquid
Solute	A mixture of a solvent and a solute
Soluble	This means 'can dissolve'
Solvent	The name for the liquid part of a solution
Solution	What happens when one substance seems to disappear when it is mixed with a liquid
Insoluble	This means 'cannot dissolve'

2. Imagine you want to dissolve two sugar cubes in a glass of water. What three things could you do to speed up the process?

3. Seawater contains salt dissolved in water. Name:

   (a) the solute;

   (b) the solvent.

Extension questions

4. Material Girl's favourite fizzy drink is cola which is a solution. Find out three main solutes, and the solvent, in cola. Try to explain why cola is bad for your teeth (look back at page 15).

5. Material Girl wants to know whether sugar crystals dissolve faster than fine grain caster sugar. Look at the experiment about dissolving sugar on the previous page and then answer the following questions:

   (a) What equipment would she need in order to carry out the experiment?

   (b) Give three things that she would need to do to ensure it was a fair test.

   (c) What should she look out for as she performs the experiment?

Hot and cold: measuring temperature

Don't forget

- Materials can be changed and sometimes the changes can happen because of heating or cooling.
- Some materials can dissolve in liquids. The amount of material that can be dissolved depends on whether the liquid is hot or cold.

How hot is it?

Imagine getting into the bath; you wouldn't want the water to be too hot or you might get burnt! People sometimes test how hot the bathwater is by putting their elbow into it. Do you think this is very reliable? Look at the diagram below and, after studying it, ask yourself whether there's a better way of measuring 'hot' than just dipping your finger in!

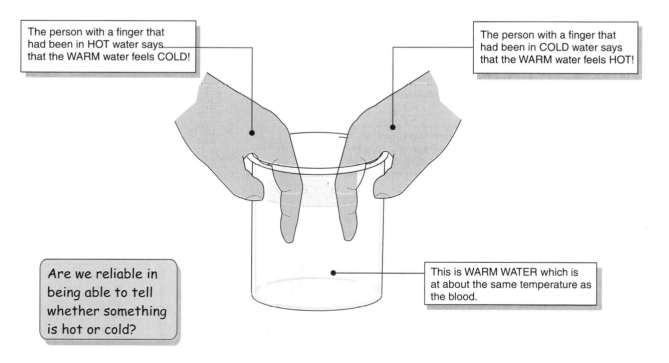

The person with a finger that had been in HOT water says that the WARM water feels COLD!

The person with a finger that had been in COLD water says that the WARM water feels HOT!

Are we reliable in being able to tell whether something is hot or cold?

This is WARM WATER which is at about the same temperature as the blood.

What do we mean by 'temperature'?

Remember that 'heat' is one kind of energy. If a material has a lot of heat (or thermal energy) we say it is **hot**, and if it has very little heat (thermal energy) we say it is **cold**. **Temperature** is a scale of numbers that we use to measure the amount of thermal energy that a material has.

Water temperature and physical changes

Water can go through two physical changes; it can change from solid ice to liquid water, and then from liquid water to steam (water vapour). These are physical changes because no new material is produced, even though the water changes the way it looks and feels. Pure water always goes through these changes at the same temperatures.

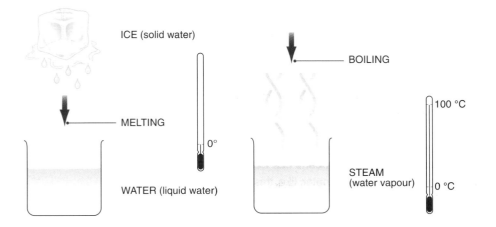

Mixtures, boiling and melting

As we now know, pure water is defined as melting at exactly 0 °C and boiling at exactly 100 °C. If there's any other material dissolved in the water, then it generally won't melt and boil at these temperatures. For example, if salt is added to water, then the water won't freeze into ice until a few degrees below 0 °C. You need to be able to measure temperatures below 0 °C, so many thermometers go down as low as −10 °C. Motorists understand all about this. When they add antifreeze to the water in their car radiator, it means the water won't freeze, even if the outside temperature falls below 0 °C.

Exercise 19.3: Temperature

1. Explain how a thermometer works.

2. What is the melting point of pure water?

3. What is the boiling point of pure water?

4. What is the body temperature of a normal healthy human?

5. (a) What do we call water when it is a solid and when it is a gas?
   (b) What happens to water when antifreeze is added to it?

Extension question

6. Use a book or the internet to find out the body temperature of a bird (the other kind of warm-blooded vertebrate).

Changing materials by heating or cooling

Don't forget

- All materials are made of tiny particles.
- Materials can be changed. Sometimes these changes alter the way a material looks or feels.

Changing state

The way a material looks and feels can be called its **state**. Scientists group materials into three states called **solids**, **liquids** or **gases** (see page 109). All materials, whether they are solids, liquids or gases, are made of tiny particles. When a material is heated, these particles speed up, and when a material is cooled the particles slow down. When these particles speed up or slow down, they sometimes change position. The particles react with each other in different ways depending on whether the material is in the state of solid, liquid or gas. This means that a material can change from solid to liquid, or from liquid to gas, as the particles move around. These changes are called **changes of state.** The words used to describe this are shown below:

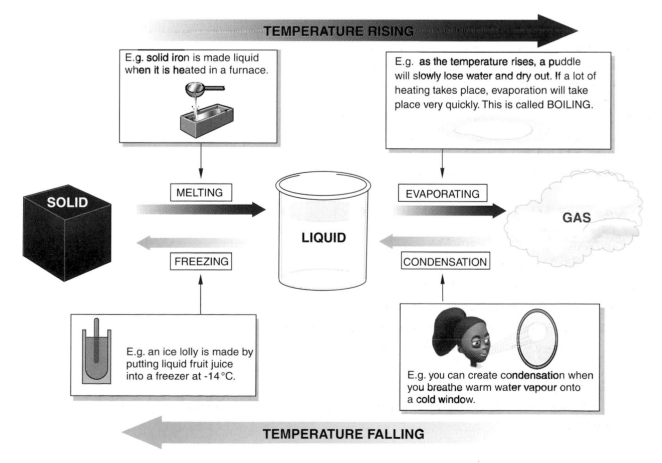

TEMPERATURE RISING

E.g. **solid iron** is made liquid when **it is he**ated in a furnace.

E.g. **as the temperature rises, a** puddle will **slowly lose water and dry out.** If a lot of heating takes place, evaporation will take place very quickly. This is called BOILING.

SOLID

MELTING

LIQUID

EVAPORATING

GAS

FREEZING

CONDENSATION

E.g. an ice lolly is made by putting liquid fruit juice into a freezer at -14°C.

E.g. you can create **condensation** when you breathe warm water **vapour** onto a **cold window.**

TEMPERATURE FALLING

The water cycle: changing materials in the environment

Think back

- Materials may go through a change of state when they are heated or cooled.
- Water can exist in three states, either as a solid, a liquid or a gas (vapour).
- When water changes from one state to another, it can change back again if the conditions are altered.

Remember that water can evaporate to form water vapour, and that water vapour can condense to form liquid water again. Don't think that these changes only take place in the laboratory or in the home; they are very important in the environment, too.

The amount of water on the Earth has stayed the same for millions of years. However, the water is constantly recycling as it changes from one state to another. Water evaporates from the sea into the air and then condenses back from the air into the sea. In between the evaporation and the condensation, the water vapour can be moved over enormous distances by winds. These natural changes in the state of water are called the **water cycle**, as shown in this diagram:

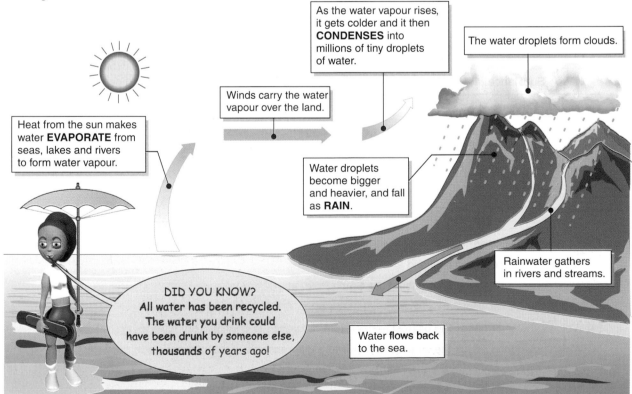

As the water vapour rises, it gets colder and it then **CONDENSES** into millions of tiny droplets of water.

The water droplets form clouds.

Winds carry the water vapour over the land.

Heat from the sun makes water **EVAPORATE** from seas, lakes and rivers to form water vapour.

Water droplets become bigger and heavier, and fall as **RAIN**.

Rainwater gathers in rivers and streams.

DID YOU KNOW?
All water has been recycled. The water you drink could have been drunk by someone else, thousands of years ago!

Water **flows back** to the sea.

The heating of water to evaporate it from the sea is caused by the Sun. Remembering how the Sun also supplied the energy for plants to make their food (see page 35), you can see why the Sun is absolutely vital for all life on Earth.

Experiments with condensation and evaporation

The amount of a substance is its mass. We can measure mass by using a weighing machine. In this experiment we can see whether the mass of water in our beaker changes when some of it evaporates away.

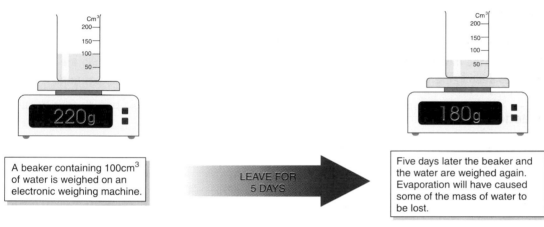

A beaker containing 100cm³ of water is weighed on an electronic weighing machine.

LEAVE FOR 5 DAYS

Five days later the beaker and the water are weighed again. Evaporation will have caused some of the mass of water to be lost.

What affects evaporation?

We can make evaporation happen more quickly by heating a wet object. We can also make it happen more quickly by blowing on it, so that 'wet' air is moved away from the object. These factors can be studied in an experiment; if it is done carefully, it can be a fair test.

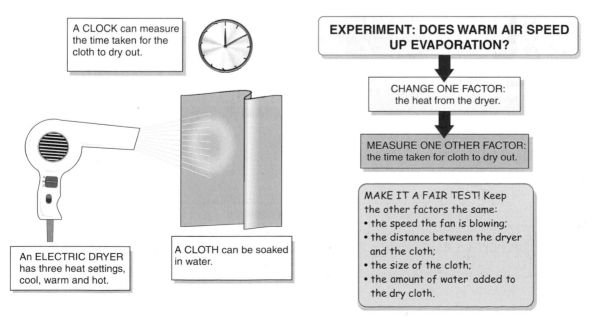

A CLOCK can measure the time taken for the cloth to dry out.

EXPERIMENT: DOES WARM AIR SPEED UP EVAPORATION?

CHANGE ONE FACTOR: the heat from the dryer.

MEASURE ONE OTHER FACTOR: the time taken for cloth to dry out.

MAKE IT A FAIR TEST! Keep the other factors the same:
• the speed the fan is blowing;
• the distance between the dryer and the cloth;
• the size of the cloth;
• the amount of water added to the dry cloth.

An ELECTRIC DRYER has three heat settings, cool, warm and hot.

A CLOTH can be soaked in water.

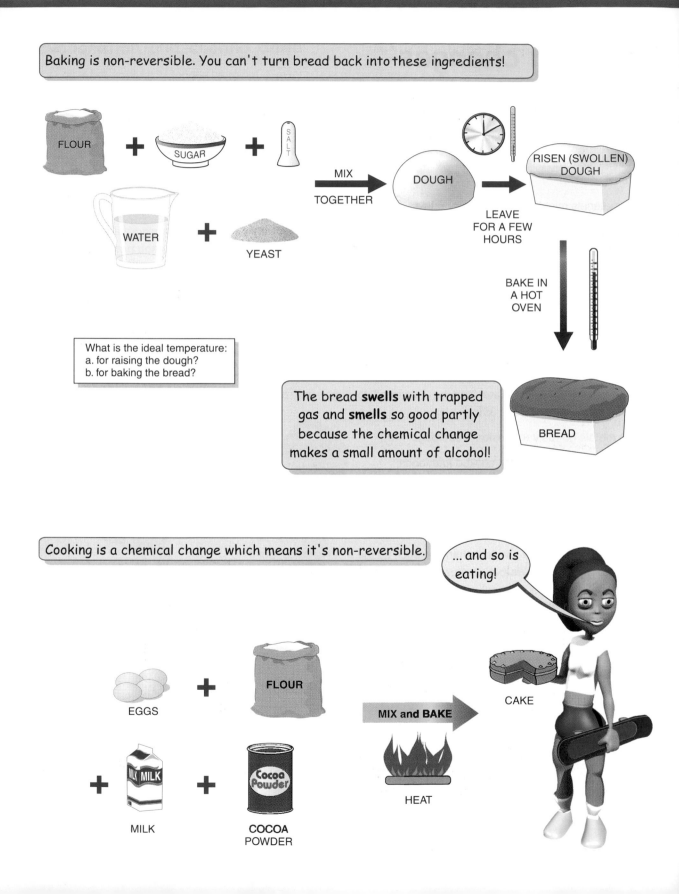

Baking is non-reversible. You can't turn bread back into these ingredients!

FLOUR + SUGAR + SALT

WATER + YEAST

MIX TOGETHER → DOUGH → RISEN (SWOLLEN) DOUGH

LEAVE FOR A FEW HOURS

BAKE IN A HOT OVEN

What is the ideal temperature:
a. for raising the dough?
b. for baking the bread?

The bread **swells** with trapped gas and **smells** so good partly because the chemical change makes a small amount of alcohol!

BREAD

Cooking is a chemical change which means it's non-reversible.

... and so is eating!

EGGS + FLOUR

MILK + COCOA POWDER

MIX and BAKE → CAKE

HEAT

A different mixture can have a rather similar result…

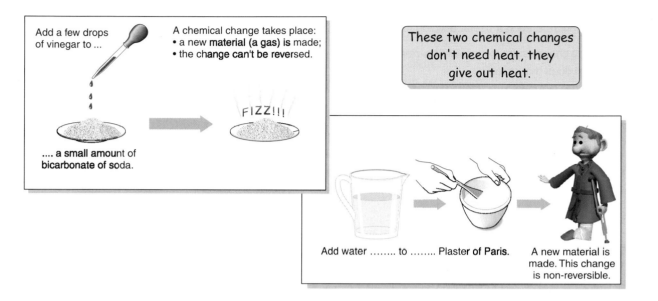

Add a few drops of vinegar to … **.... a small amount of bicarbonate of soda.**

A chemical change takes place:
• a new **material (a gas) is** made;
• the change can't be reversed.

FIZZ!!!

These two chemical changes don't need heat, they give out heat.

Add water …….. to …….. Plaster **of Paris.**

A new material is made. This change is non-reversible.

Some chemical changes don't need heat

Not all chemical changes need heat to occur. Some chemical changes even give out heat! Two changes that give out heat, and can easily be tried in a school laboratory, are shown in the diagrams above.

Making concrete is a useful chemical change.

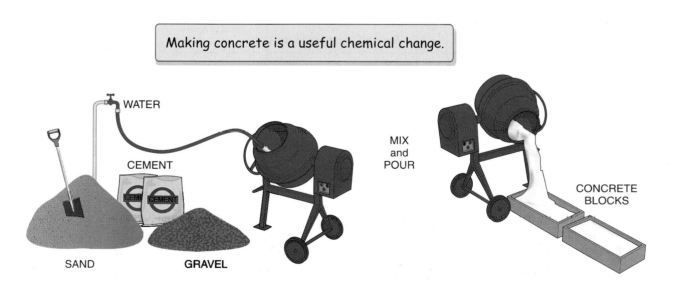

WATER

CEMENT

SAND

GRAVEL

MIX and POUR

CONCRETE BLOCKS

How can rusting be prevented?

Both air and water are needed for iron or steel to rust. Rusting will not take place if either air or water cannot reach the iron or steel. There are several different ways of keeping air or water away from iron and steel:

You can prevent rusting by putting a **coating** on iron and steel to keep out air and water.

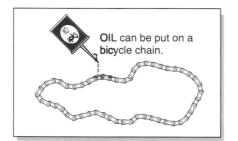

OIL can be put on a **bicy**cle chain.

A ZINC COATING (GALVANISING) can be used on steel buckets and screws.

A coating of TIN can be put on cans made from steel.

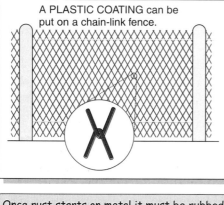

A PLASTIC COATING can be put on a chain-link fence.

Once rust starts on metal it must be rubbed away (usually with sandpaper) before the bare metal is carefully repainted.

Painting a protective covering on a steel drum.

Other metals do not rust, although they still take part in chemical changes. These changes, called corrosion, are more likely to occur if the air is polluted. Corrosion often leaves a thin layer of a differently-coloured material on the surface of a metal. A common example of this occurs with the metal called bronze. Bronze is often used to make statues, and turns green from corrosion.

A bronze statue of Johannes Gutenberg who invented a type of printing press. He produced his first book in 1456.

Exercise 19.7: Rusting

1. Fill in the missing words to complete this paragraph.

Rusting is a chemical .... that can damage .... and .... Iron only goes rusty

if both .... and .... are present. Metals such as .... do not rust but they

can suffer from .... This occurs much more quickly if there is a lot of .... in the air.

2. You notice a small spot of rust on the frame of your bicycle. What can you do to stop it from spreading?

3. What stops a baked bean tin from going rusty?

Extension question

4. A scientist was trying to work out what caused rusting. She had heard that water and air were needed, but she also thought that rusting would be worse if the water were warm and salty. She set up five tubes like the ones in this diagram.

1. Water + air

2. Salty water + air

3. Warm water + air

4. Warm, salty water + air

Layer of oil

5. Warm boiled salty, water

After 10 days she took the nails out of the tubes, and measured how much of the nail was covered in rust. She wrote down the results in a table, giving a figure of 0 if there was no rust and 1 if the nail was completely covered in rust.

Tube number	Amount of rust
1	0.4
2	0.6
3	0.7
4	1.0
5	

(a) Draw a bar chart of these results, using graph paper or a computer program.

(b) Which had the biggest effect on rusting, salt or warmth? Give a reason for your answer.

(c) She did not write in the result for the fifth tube. What do you think the result would be? Give a reason for your answer.

Fire hazard

We try to control burning fuel firstly, so that we don't waste any of the heat and secondly, so that it doesn't put us in any danger. Sometimes things go wrong and the burning gets out of control. If this happens, forests can be destroyed, buildings can burn down and humans may be killed. Firefighters try their hardest to put fires out before they cause any damage.

The combustion triangle shown opposite shows the three things needed for burning. The burning will stop if any of these things is removed. Firefighters have three ways of putting out a fire.

- **Getting rid of the fuel**: for example, by pulling burning wood away from the fire, or turning the gas off at the mains.

- **Getting rid of the heat**: for example, by cooling down the fire with water, they can stop any more fuel from catching alight.

- **Cutting off the supply of air**: by covering the fire with foam, earth or a fire blanket, for example.

Fire fighters hosing a fire at a piano factory

It is not always safe to use water on a fire because:

- **Water conducts electricity**, so if the fire is in an electric appliance, someone might get an electric shock. You should use a foam fire extinguisher.

- **Water and fat don't mix**, so if the fire is in burning oil or fat, the oil might splatter and spit. This could spread the fire, or burn someone standing nearby. You should use a fire blanket.

Slow burning in the body

All living organisms need to carry out life processes (see page 5). These life processes need energy, which as we have learned is released from the food that is taken in or made. This energy is released by a special kind of slow burning (called **respiration**). You can tell that it's going on because when we breathe out, our breath contains carbon dioxide and water.

Exercise 19.8: Burning

1. Which one of these is not a fossil fuel?

   NATURAL GAS, WOOD, OIL, COAL

2. Some people say that burning wood is a waste. What are the useful products for humans?

3. How can you tell that burning is a chemical change?

4. Give a reason why covering burning wood with a blanket will put out the fire.

Extension questions

5. A scientist wanted to find out how much heat energy is given out when fuels burn. He took different fuels and burned them and then measured the heat energy released. Here are the results:

Type of fuel	Units of heat released	Amount of fuel burned in grams	Units of heat from 100 grams of fuel
Coal	40	60	
Gas	54	80	
Paraffin	36	50	
Petrol	60	50	
Diesel oil	54	75	

   (a) Copy out the table. Complete the final column of the table. Why is it important to complete this final column?

   (b) The scientist always used the same amount of air for his experiment. Why is this important?

   (c) Draw a bar chart of the results from the final column. Which is the most useful heating fuel?

6. Give three good reasons why a human needs a supply of air.

It is very difficult completely to separate the solid and liquid by **decanting**. To complete the separation of the solid and liquid, it is best also to separate them by using a **filter**.

Separating a solid from a liquid: filtration

A filter is a layer with many tiny holes in it. The tiny holes let the liquid through but keep the solid back. A filter is like a very fine sieve, and indeed some filters look just like sieves. A good example is a colander which is used to hold back cooked vegetables from the water they were boiled in, or a tea strainer used to keep tea leaves out of a cup of tea.

Filtering can separate solids from a liquid

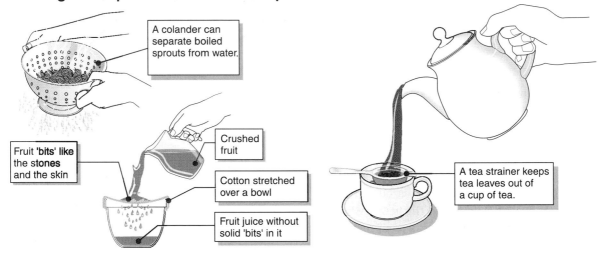

A colander can separate boiled sprouts from water.

Fruit 'bits' like the stones and the skin

Crushed fruit

Cotton stretched over a bowl

Fruit juice without solid 'bits' in it

A tea strainer keeps tea leaves out of a cup of tea.

Many filters are made from paper, and these can keep back really small particles of solid. Using filter paper is very important in scientific experiments.

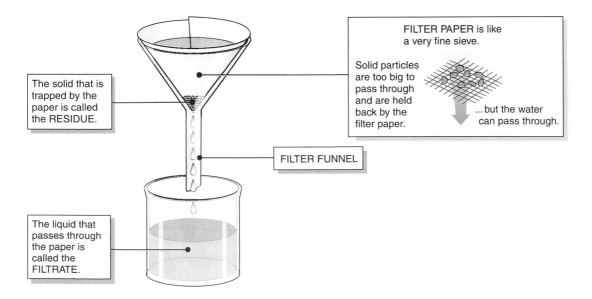

The solid that is trapped by the paper is called the RESIDUE.

FILTER PAPER is like a very fine sieve.

Solid particles are too big to pass through and are held back by the filter paper.

...but the water can pass through.

FILTER FUNNEL

The liquid that passes through the paper is called the FILTRATE.

Exercise 20.1: Separating mixtures

1. What is the difference between a pure substance and a mixture?

2. Copy out and complete this paragraph.

A sieve can be used to separate a mixture of different .... depending on the ....
of the particles. Filter paper acts like a very fine .... and we can use the technique of
.... to separate a mixture of liquid and solid. The ....
left behind on the filter paper is called the residue, and the liquid that goes through the filter paper is called the
....

3. Explain what is meant by the following and give an example of each:
   (a) filtering
   (b) decanting
   (c) sieving

4. Material Girl mixes chalk and warm water together in a beaker. Draw a simple labelled diagram of the
   equipment she would use to remove the solid from the liquid by filtration.

5 Give a good reason why we might want to separate the different materials in a mixture.

Extension question

6. A frozen food factory made a terrible mistake, and mixed up the frozen peas with the frozen sprouts.
   How could they separate them again? Draw a diagram to help you.

The process of separating a mixture

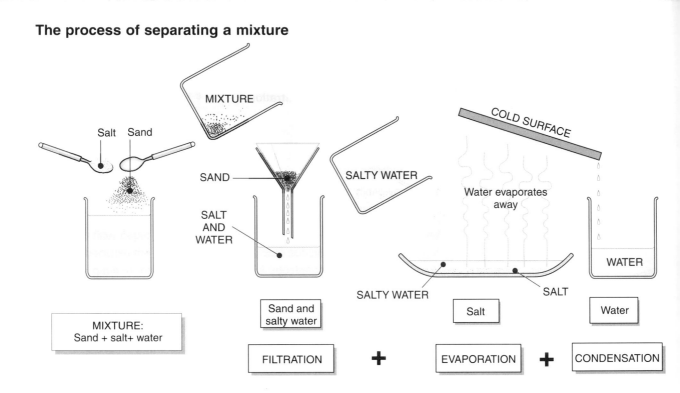

Exercise 20.2: Separating mixtures

1. What is the difference between a solvent and a solute?

2. What is the difference between a soluble and an insoluble substance?

3. Match up the following words with their meanings:

   filtration   condensation   evaporation   separation.

   MEANINGS

   (a) a change from a vapour to a liquid

   (b) separating the solid parts of a mixture from the liquid parts

   (c) getting the different substances out of a mixture

   (d) changing a liquid to a gas or vapour

Extension questions

4. Describe how you would separate salt from pepper (here's a clue: salt dissolves in water but pepper doesn't).

5. Material Girl makes another mixture by adding sand, salt and tea leaves to a beaker of warm water. She then decides she wants to separate all the substances out again. Design an experiment and describe the four stages she would have to go through in order to achieve this.

Physical processes

And finally, we turn to our third section in which Professor Particle will help you to understand physical processes.

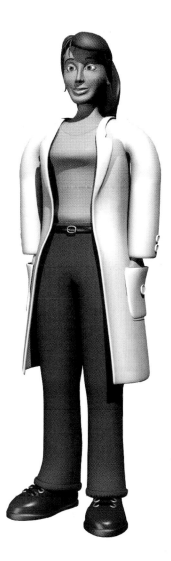

Round and round: electrical circuits

You will remember from earlier in your work (see page 21) that blood flows in blood vessels around your body. The blood is pumped from the heart, round the body and then back to the heart. We say it completes a **circuit** of the body. Electricity flows in a similar sort of way around a circuit.

- Electricity flows through **wires** (also called **leads**) instead of vessels. These wires act as **electrical conductors** (see page 115).

- Electricity begins and ends a circuit at a **power source** such as a cell (battery).

- Electricity flowing around a circuit is called the **electric current**.

Whether an electrical appliance uses the mains or a battery, the appliance won't work unless it is part of a **complete circuit**.

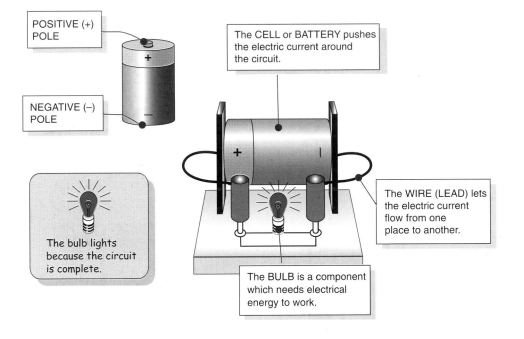

POSITIVE (+) POLE

NEGATIVE (−) POLE

The CELL or BATTERY pushes the electric current around the circuit.

The WIRE (LEAD) lets the electric current flow from one place to another.

The bulb lights because the circuit is complete.

The BULB is a component which needs electrical energy to work.

How to connect up a complete circuit

A cell (battery) pushes the electric current around a circuit. Each cell has a **positive** end (+) and a **negative** end (−). These are called the **poles** or **terminals** of the cell. In order to connect up a complete circuit, you need to:

- attach a lead to the positive pole of the battery;

- connect the other end of this lead to a component, such as a bulb. If the component has a positive or negative side, connect the lead to the positive side;

- attach another lead from the negative pole of the component to the negative pole of the battery.

You should now have a complete circuit.

Exercise 21.1: Circuits

1. What are the three things needed for a complete circuit?

2. Give three rules for working safely with electricity.

3. Describe what a cell (battery) is and what it does.

Extension question

4. This question deals with electrical appliances that you could find in your home or school. Make a list of ten different appliances, and use the list to complete a table like this one.

Appliance	Is it powered by mains or battery?	It converts electrical energy to ...

Bulbs resist the flow of electricity. In fact the more bulbs there are, the lower the current. If there are two bulbs in a series circuit, each bulb is much dimmer than if there is only one. Other components in a series circuit, such as buzzers and motors, will also reduce the current.

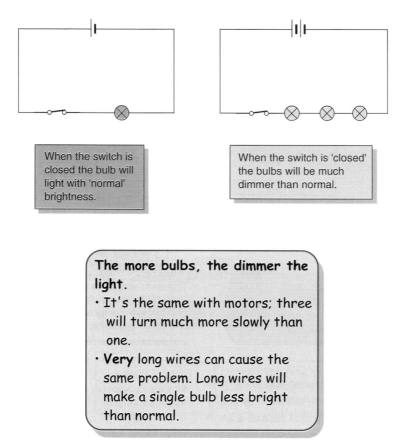

When the switch is closed the bulb will light with 'normal' brightness.

When the switch is 'closed' the bulbs will be much dimmer than normal.

The more bulbs, the dimmer the light.
- It's the same with motors; three will turn much more slowly than one.
- **Very** long wires can cause the same problem. Long wires will make a single bulb less bright than normal.

What is resistance?

Resistance is a measure of how difficult it is for current to flow through a circuit. A material like plastic or glass has so much resistance that electric current does not flow through it at all. Materials that do not allow electricity to flow through them are called **insulators** (see page 115).

Exercise 21.3: Problems with circuits

1. Look at these two circuits. Which part of each circuit will the current miss out?

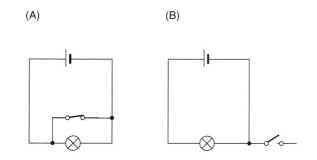

(A)   (B)

2. Fill in the gaps to complete this sentence.
   In a circuit, more cells will make the bulb glow .... and more bulbs will make the bulbs glow
   ....

3. Make a list of the type of faults that stop an electrical circuit from working.

Extension questions

4. Look at the diagram of the faulty torch on page 172. Draw a circuit diagram to show the faults.

5. (a) Draw four simple circuits as follows:

   (i)   a circuit with one cell and one bulb in which the bulb lights to normal brightness;

   (ii) a circuit with one cell and two bulbs in series;

   (iii) a circuit with two cells and one bulb;

   (iv) a circuit with three cells and one bulb.

   (b) Arrange your four circuits (i) - (iv) in order of brightness, starting with the dimmest.

   (c) What would happen if one of the bulbs in circuit (ii) broke?

   (d) What would you add to circuit (ii) so that the bulbs light to normal brightness?

6. Draw a simple circuit to represent a battery-powered door buzzer.

Friction

- Forces can act as a push or a pull.
- Forces can affect the way that objects move.

Moving objects often slow down by themselves, even if we don't want them to. These objects slow down because there is a force acting on them. The force is acting in the opposite direction to the way they are moving. This force is called **friction**.

- Car tyres can push against the surface of the road, so the car can move forward.

Friction can be a nuisance!

AIR and BODY: This will make the bike and rider slow down.

CHAIN and GEARS: friction here makes pedalling very hard work.

TYRES and GROUND: Grip means that the bike will 'stick' to the ground unless the rider keeps pedalling.

Friction can be useful!

HANDLEBARS GRIPS and GLOVES: Easier to hold on.

PEDALS and SOLES OF SHOES: Feet won't slip off the pedals.

BRAKES and WHEEL RIMS: Means that the bike can be stopped.

TYRES and GROUND: Grip means that the bike can be pedalled forward.

WITHOUT FRICTION YOU COULDN'T TIE A KNOT

Friction is a force that tries to stop two things from sliding over each other. Sometimes friction is *useful*:

- Brake blocks can squeeze against a bicycle wheel rim, so that the bike slows down.
- Shoes can grip the floor, so that you don't slip when you try to walk.
- Knots in ropes stay tied.
- Friction lets us strike matches on a matchbox.

… but sometimes it is a *nuisance:*

- it slows moving things down, and extra force is needed to keep them moving; and
- it can heat things up and can damage the moving surfaces.

How to reduce friction

Friction is caused by tiny bumps between surfaces. These bumps are just like tiny pieces of sandpaper, and they stop the surfaces from moving. Friction can be reduced in the following ways:

- Smoothing off the surfaces because smooth surfaces have less friction than rough ones.
- Adding a substance that keeps the surfaces slightly apart. This kind of substance is called a **lubricant.** Good examples of lubricants are grease and oil.

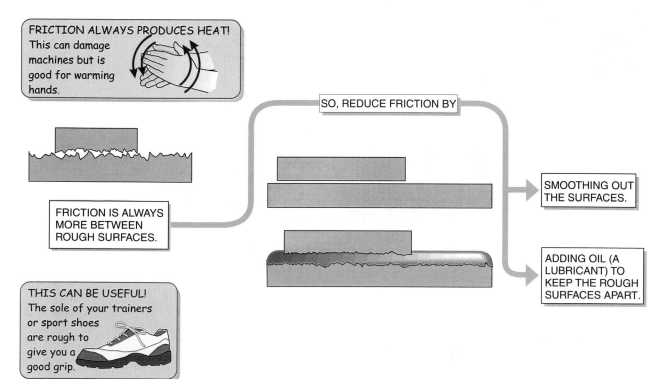

FRICTION ALWAYS PRODUCES HEAT! This can damage machines but is good for warming hands.

SO, REDUCE FRICTION BY

FRICTION IS ALWAYS MORE BETWEEN ROUGH SURFACES.

SMOOTHING OUT THE SURFACES.

ADDING OIL (A LUBRICANT) TO KEEP THE ROUGH SURFACES APART.

THIS CAN BE USEFUL! The sole of your trainers or sport shoes are rough to give you a good grip.

Air resistance is a kind of friction

Air resistance (sometimes called **drag**) is a kind of friction between a moving object and the air. This kind of drag acts on you as you cycle along the road. The amount of drag can be reduced by making the object more **streamlined**. Streamlining will allow an object to travel faster through the air.

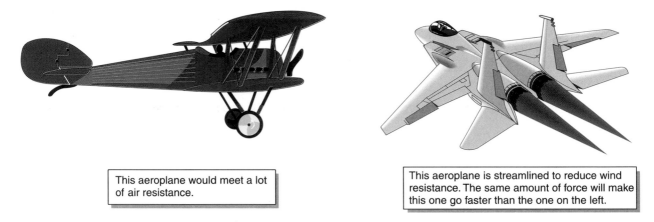

This aeroplane would meet a lot of air resistance.

This aeroplane is streamlined to reduce wind resistance. The same amount of force will make this one go faster than the one on the left.

To travel slowly through the air, you need a large surface area, and indeed this is exactly how a parachute works. A parachutist uses the parachute to slow down his/her movement through the air and to try to balance the effects of gravity (see page 186).

Measuring friction

Friction is a kind of force, so it is measured using a forcemeter. The way that this is done is shown in the diagram below. Measurements of friction between different kinds of surface must be done as a **fair test**.

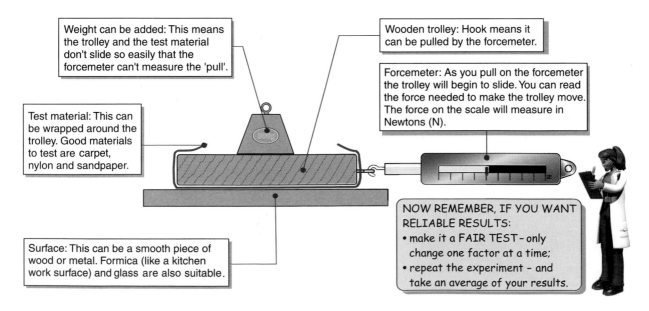

Weight can be added: This means the trolley and the test material don't slide so easily that the forcemeter can't measure the 'pull'.

Wooden trolley: Hook means it can be pulled by the forcemeter.

Test material: This can be wrapped around the trolley. Good materials to test are carpet, nylon and sandpaper.

Forcemeter: As you pull on the forcemeter the trolley will begin to slide. You can read the force needed to make the trolley move. The force on the scale will measure in Newtons (N).

Surface: This can be a smooth piece of wood or metal. Formica (like a kitchen work surface) and glass are also suitable.

NOW REMEMBER, IF YOU WANT RELIABLE RESULTS:
• make it a FAIR TEST – only change one factor at a time;
• repeat the experiment – and take an average of your results.

Exercise 22.3: Friction

1. Write down two friction forces that would slow down a bicycle.

2. Give two examples of times when friction is useful.

3. Give two things that always happen when friction takes place.

4. What is air resistance?

5. Look at the two aeroplanes on the opposite page. Which one would face the greatest amount of air resistance as it taxied along the runway before take-off?

Extension questions

6. Look at the diagram showing how to measure friction, on the previous page. Imagine that you are a scientist studying friction between wood and other materials. Write down:
   (a) what you would be changing;
   (b) what you would be measuring; and
   (c) what you would need to keep constant.

7. Professor Particle wants to try different test materials to see how much friction there is with the wheels of a toy car. She set up her 'u'-shaped track.

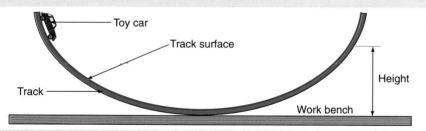

   (a) Which of the following would achieve a fair test? Give reasons for your answer.
   (i) Using two cars, one with steel wheels and one with rubber wheels. The test material is a piece of cotton.
   (ii) Using a car with rubber wheels and three different test materials: writing paper, carpet and sandpaper.
   (iii) Using two cars and two different types of sandpaper as the test material, one smooth and one very rough.
   (iv) Using two different pieces of woolen cloth, one car and two different 'u'-shaped tracks.

   (b) Professor Particle decides to use a car with rubber wheels, one 'u'-shaped track and four different materials: carpet, writing paper, a woolen blanket and some rough sandpaper. For each test she released the car from the same place on the track and measured the height it reached on the opposite side of the 'u'-shaped track from the work bench. The results are shown below:

Type of material	Mean height reached in cm (after 10 tries)
Carpet	12
Writing paper	40
Woolen blanket	26
Rough sandpaper	32

   (i) Which surface provided the least friction?
   (ii) Which surface provided the most friction?
   (iii) Why did Professor Particle repeat the experiment ten times for each material?

The force of gravity

Remember

- A force can be a push or a pull.
- Any object that is not changing speed is being acted on by balanced forces.

Gravity and the Earth

Gravity is a **force of attraction,** in other words, a **pull** between any two objects.

- The size of the force depends on the **size of the objects**. The *bigger* the objects, the *bigger* the gravitational force of attraction between them.
- The size of the force depends on how **close to each other the objects are**. The *closer* the objects, the *bigger* the force of gravity between them.

The Earth is a large object, so puts a 'pull' force on other objects that are near it. The force of gravity has a direction, and this direction is towards the centre of the Earth.

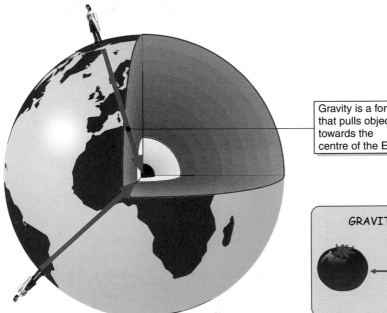

Gravity is a force that pulls objects towards the centre of the Earth.

GRAVITY EXISTS BETWEEN OBJECTS.

Even very small objects, like two tomatoes, are pulled towards each other. The force is very small so it would be really difficult to measure it.

There are two important things to remember about gravity.

- Gravity will pull an object towards the centre of the Earth whether the object is in the air, standing on the ground or in water.
- Most places on the surface of the Earth are almost the same distance from the centre of the Earth. Because of this, the force of gravity is almost exactly the same all over the Earth. You need to get a long way away from the Earth (about 387 000 km!) before you notice any real reduction in the force of gravity.

Beating the force of gravity

The Earth is very tightly packed with materials like rocks, so gravity can't pull us through to the centre of the Earth. Gravity does tend to pull us until we reach the Earth's surface, though. But we can beat gravity in three ways:

1. **By exerting a force In the opposite direction**. This could involve using a rocket motor which burns fuel to push it against the force of gravity.

Beating gravity

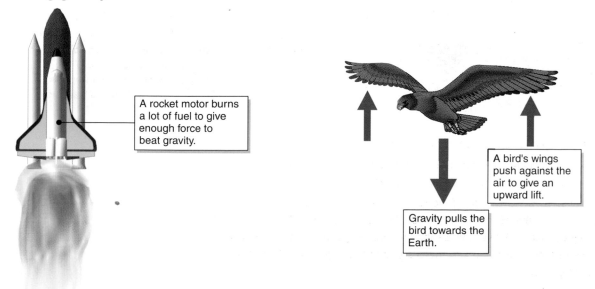

A rocket motor burns a lot of fuel to give enough force to beat gravity.

Gravity pulls the bird towards the Earth.

A bird's wings push against the air to give an upward lift.

2. Using an upward force to support you. This is an example of a **reaction** force. This could involve something as simple as sitting up in a tree house.

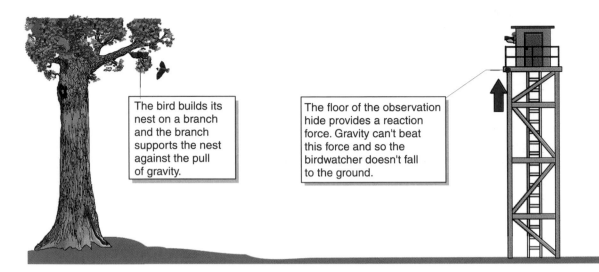

The bird builds its nest on a branch and the branch supports the nest against the pull of gravity.

The floor of the observation hide provides a reaction force. Gravity can't beat this force and so the birdwatcher doesn't fall to the ground.

3. Using the upthrust of water. Water pushes up against objects that are floating in it. This cancels out some of the force of gravity pulling the objects towards the centre of the Earth. An object will float when the force of gravity is balanced by the upthrust of the water.

We can see another example of opposing the force of gravity if we look at a parachutist. We just need to remember that forces are balanced when an object is moving at a steady speed.

Professor Particle makes a parachute jump

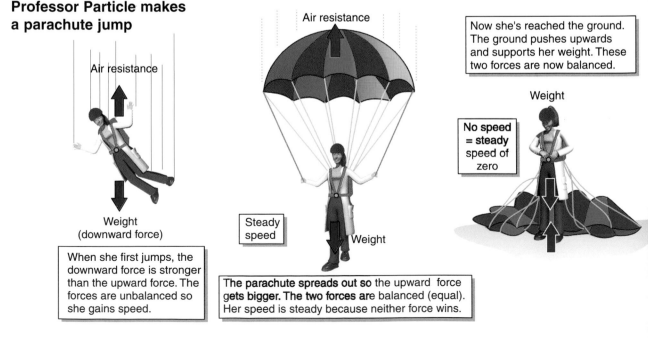

Air resistance

Weight (downward force)

When she first jumps, the downward force is stronger than the upward force. The forces are unbalanced so she gains speed.

Air resistance

Steady speed

Weight

The parachute spreads out so the upward force gets bigger. The two forces are balanced (equal). Her speed is steady because neither force wins.

Now she's reached the ground. The ground pushes upwards and supports her weight. These two forces are now balanced.

Weight

No speed = steady speed of zero

Measuring gravity

The force of gravity acting on objects can make them feel very heavy. This 'heaviness' as a result of gravity is the **weight** of an object. Because weight is a force, we can also measure it by using a forcemeter. The weight of an object should be measured in **Newtons**.

Using a forcemeter to measure weight

You can hang a weight on the hook at the bottom of a forcemeter. When the spring inside the forcemeter is stretched, it tries to pull back towards its normal length. The weight hangs in one position because this pull of the spring equals the downward pull of gravity on the weight. The two forces are balanced.

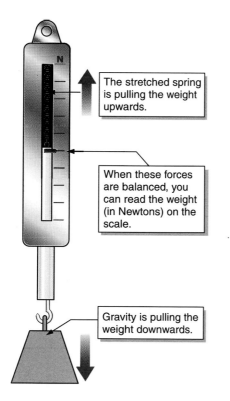

The stretched spring is pulling the weight upwards.

When these forces are balanced, you can read the weight (in Newtons) on the scale.

Gravity is pulling the weight downwards.

Exercise 22.4: Gravity

1. Complete these sentences.

   Weight is a force and is measured in .... It is caused by .... acting on an object.

2. How do birds overcome the force of gravity?

3. Why is there less force of gravity between two apples than between the Earth and one apple?

Extension questions

4. Why do astronauts need to wear heavy boots when they walk on the Moon?

5. Two students hung a spring from a strong support alongside a long ruler. They measured where the bottom of the spring was when there was no weight added to the spring, this was the starting point. They then added different weights to the spring and measured where the bottom of the spring reached on the scale. They worked out the stretch of the spring by taking away the starting point from the finishing point each time.

   Here are their results.

Added weight (grams)	Position of spring (millimetres)	Amount of stretch (millimetres)
0	12	0
10	22	
20	35	
30	48	
40	60	
50	73	
60	85	
70	97	85
80	110	
90	122	
100	136	
110	149	
120	160	

   (a) Complete the table by working out the amount of stretch for each added weight.

   (b) Plot a graph of the added weight against the stretch of the spring.

   (c) What is the pattern in these results?

Chapter 23
Light and light sources

Light is made of rays that your eyes can detect. If there is no light, in other words when it's completely dark, you can't see at all. The light we need in order to see objects comes from **light sources**. These light sources include the Sun, stars, light bulbs and burning objects. Because a light source gives off its own light, we say it is **luminous**.

Light sources are luminous, which means they give out light

Stars

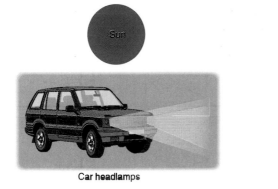

Car headlamps

A campfire

Some other objects look as though they are light sources because they are so bright. These objects look bright to us because they reflect light into our eyes from another light source. These **reflectors** include the Moon, mirrors and even this page.

These objects are not luminous, even though we can see them

The Moon reflects light from the sun.

THIS WRITING

You can read this because light is reflected off the paper.

The shiny surface at the back of headlights.

Shiny objects, like a diamond and gold ring.

Properties of light

Light has some very important properties.

- **Light always travels in straight lines**. This means that we can't see an object if there is anything in the way of these straight lines. When we try to draw the way light is travelling, we always use straight lines.

Light travels in a straight line

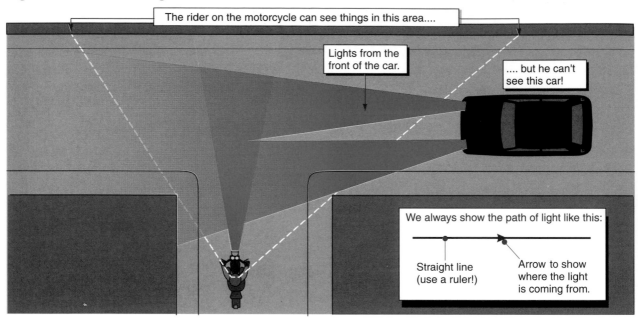

The rider on the motorcycle can see things in this area....

Lights from the front of the car.

.... but he can't see this car!

We always show the path of light like this:

Straight line (use a ruler!)

Arrow to show where the light is coming from.

- If something gets in the way of light, a **shadow** is formed (see page 186).
- **Light travels very fast**. It is very difficult to measure the speed of light, but scientists have measured that light travels at 300 000 km per second.

Light travels fast

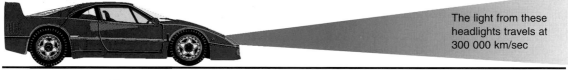

The light from these headlights travels at 300 000 km/sec

This Formula 1 racing car travels at around 1/15th km/sec.

Using our eyes – how we see things

Remember, we see things when light enters our eyes. The light can come:

- directly from the source to our eyes, for example light from a burning match;
- when light from a source is reflected from (in other words, bounces off) an object.

It doesn't matter where the light comes from, we won't see it unless;

- the light can reach our eye in a straight line from the object; or unless
- the light rays can actually enter our eye.

How we see things

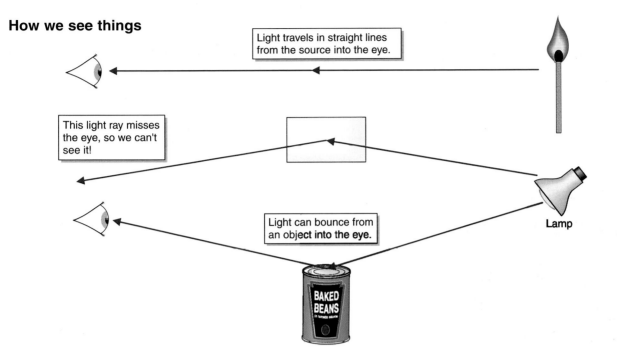

Light travels in straight lines from the source into the eye.

This light ray misses the eye, so we can't see it!

Light can bounce from an object into the eye.

Lamp

BAKED BEANS

Exercise 23.1: Light

1. Complete this paragraph.

   You can't see an object unless there is some ....
   The objects you can see are either .... (giving out light) or .... light into
   your eyes. Light is made up of .... and always travels in ....
   A .... is formed because light cannot pass through solid objects.

2. Which of these objects is a light source?

   THE MOON, THE SUN, A TORCH, A BURNING CANDLE, THE SILVER PAPER WRAPPER FROM A
   CHOCOLATE BAR, THE CHROME RADIATOR GRILLE ON A SPORTS CAR.

3. The Sun is a luminous object. Explain what is meant by the term luminous.

4. During a power cut electric lights go off. Write down three different things you could use to provide you with
   light during a power cut.

Extension questions

5. Draw a diagram to explain why you can see your watch by moonlight. It isn't a luminous watch!

6. Use straight lines to explain why you can still see a cat in the shadow behind a house. This is definitely not
   a luminous cat!

Shadows

Professor Particle doesn't want you to forget that:

- light travels in straight lines;
- light cannot pass through solid objects.

Light can pass through some materials

Light travels in straight lines, but cannot pass through all materials.

- **Transparent materials** are materials where light can pass straight through. The light isn't changed when it passes through the material. This means that you can clearly see objects that are behind these materials or inside boxes made of these materials.

Transparent materials

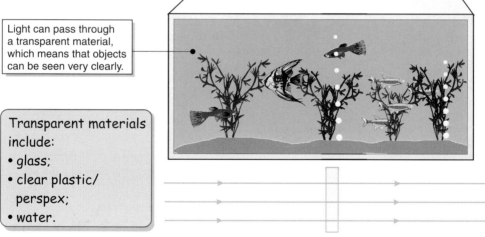

Light can pass through a transparent material, which means that objects can be seen very clearly.

Transparent materials include:
- glass;
- clear plastic/ perspex;
- water.

Light rays pass straight through a transparent material.

- **Translucent materials** allow light to pass through, but they change some of the light rays. This means that you can't get a clear picture of an object if it is behind a translucent material.

Translucent materials

Translucent materials include:
- some plastic;
- tissue paper;
- (e.g. frosted glass in a bathroom window).

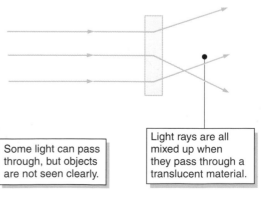

Some light can pass through, but objects are not seen clearly.

Light rays are all mixed up when they pass through a translucent material.

- **Opaque materials** are materials that stop all light from passing through. This means that none of the light rays can get from one side of the material to the other. You can't see an object through an opaque material.

Opaque materials

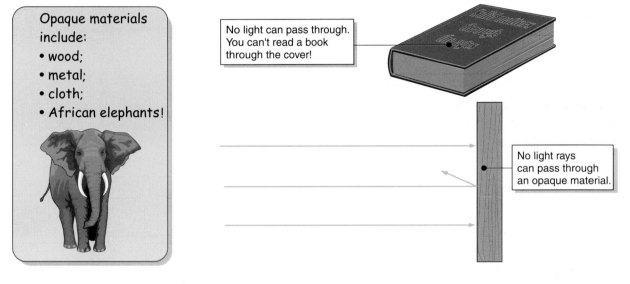

Opaque materials include:
- wood;
- metal;
- cloth;
- African elephants!

No light can pass through. You can't read a book through the cover!

No light rays can pass through an opaque material.

How shadows are formed

When light rays from a source are blocked, a **shadow** is formed. This can be shown by carefully drawing a diagram of how light rays fall on an opaque material.

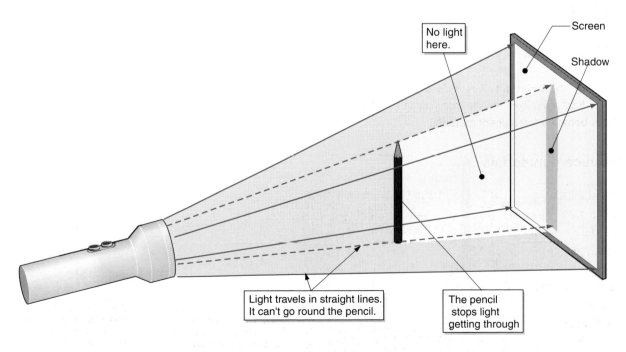

No light here.

Screen

Shadow

Light travels in straight lines. It can't go round the pencil.

The pencil stops light getting through

Two things affect the way shadows are made:

- shadows are **larger** if the object is close to the light source;
- shadows are **shorter** if the light source is almost overhead.

You can study each of these effects by carrying out proper **fair tests**. These fair tests are described in the two diagrams below:

Changing the size of a shadow

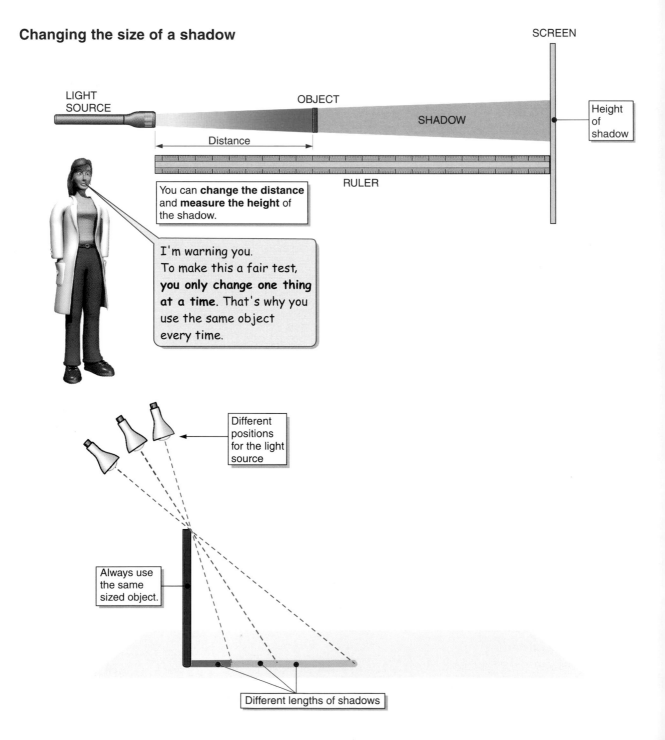

SCREEN

LIGHT SOURCE

OBJECT

SHADOW

Height of shadow

Distance

RULER

You can **change the distance** and **measure the height** of the shadow.

I'm warning you. To make this a fair test, **you only change one thing at a time**. That's why you use the same object every time.

Different positions for the light source

Always use the same sized object.

Different lengths of shadows

Exercise 23.2: Shadows

1. (a) Give an example of a transparent material.
   (b) Say what it might be used for and why.

2. (a) Give an example of a translucent material.
   (b) Say what it might be used for and why.

3. (a) Give an example of an opaque material.
   (b) Say what it might be used for and why.

4. Draw a diagram to show how a shadow forms behind a garden fence on a sunny day. Use a ruler to draw straight lines.

Extension questions

5. Look at this diagram. Carefully draw light rays to show how a shadow forms on the screen. Measure the height of the shadow.

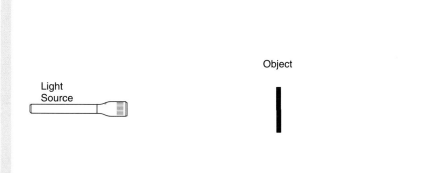

6. Professor Particle decided to carry out an experiment on shadows. She changed the distance between the light source and the object, and then measured the height of the shadow on the screen. Here are her results.

Distance between light source and object in millimetres	Height of shadow in millimetres
20	90
40	60
60	30
80	15
100	9
120	6

(a) Draw a graph of the results.
(b) What is the pattern of these results?
(c) How big would the shadow be if the light source was 50 mm from the object?

Mirrors and the reflection of light

Don't forget

- Some objects are luminous which means we can see them because they give out their own light.
- We can see other objects because they reflect the light that shines on them.
- Light rays travel in straight lines.

Mirrors reflect light back at the same angle

When light hits a shiny surface, the light rays bounce off the surface. We say that the light rays are **reflected**. Shiny surfaces reflect light rays back at exactly the same angle as they arrived.

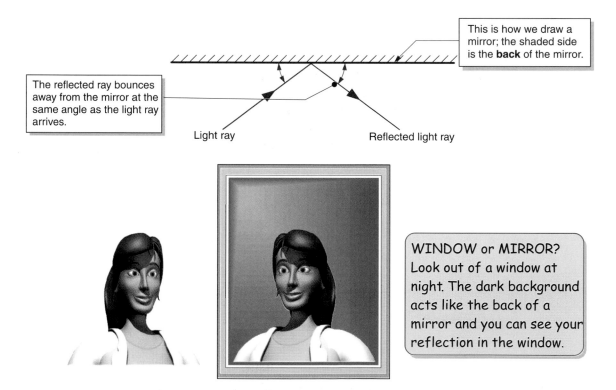

This is how we draw a mirror; the shaded side is the **back** of the mirror.

The reflected ray bounces away from the mirror at the same angle as the light ray arrives.

Light ray

Reflected light ray

WINDOW or MIRROR? Look out of a window at night. The dark background acts like the back of a mirror and you can see your reflection in the window.

We can use almost any shiny surface to act like a mirror. Dull or rough surfaces are no use as mirrors because they don't let the light bounce back without mixing up the light rays. There are many other surfaces that do reflect light but don't act as mirrors (paper is a very good example of this kind of material).

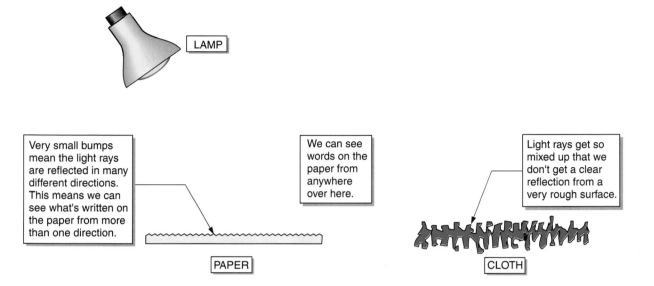

LAMP

Very small bumps mean the light rays are reflected in many different directions. This means we can see what's written on the paper from more than one direction.

We can see words on the paper from anywhere over here.

Light rays get so mixed up that we don't get a clear reflection from a very rough surface.

PAPER

CLOTH

Looking in a mirror

When you look into a flat mirror, you see objects back-to-front (**reversed**). This means that you would see any writing back-to-front, and so it would be difficult to read! Sometimes it's really important that you are able to read a word in a mirror. If an ambulance or a fire engine drives up behind your car, you need to know exactly what it is. Because of the need to do this the words 'AMBULANCE' or 'FIRE ENGINE' are painted back to front on the front of these vehicles. This means a car driver will see the words the right way round in the car's rear view mirror.

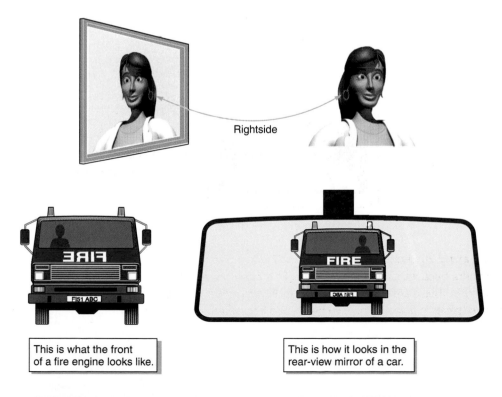

Rightside

This is what the front of a fire engine looks like.

This is how it looks in the rear-view mirror of a car.

Using a periscope

A **periscope** uses two mirrors to let you see round or over an object. Periscopes let the commander of a submarine see what is going on on the surface of the water. They were first used by soldiers in the First World War. They let the soldiers see out of the trenches without taking the risk of being shot.

A periscope

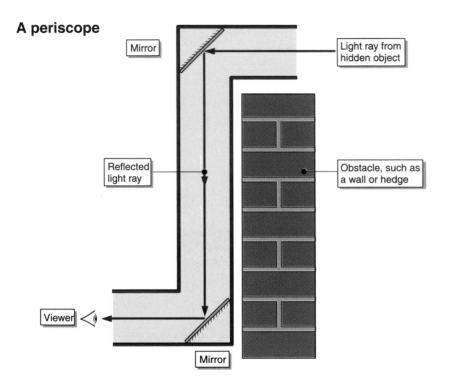

Exercise 23.3: Reflection

1. Draw a diagram to show how you could use a periscope to watch a sports match over a fence.

2. Look at this clock. It is viewed in a mirror. What time is it?

3. Write your name and address on a piece of paper, so that it is the right way round in a mirror.

Extension questions

4. Make a list of five reflecting surfaces from your home. Choose one surface that is normally transparent but sometimes can be reflecting (think carefully).

5. Look back to the diagram on page 192. Where would you put a mirror, so that the motorcyclist could see the car?

Chapter 24
Vibration and sound

Making sound

There are many different sounds, but they all have one thing in common. Sounds only happen when something vibrates. When something **vibrates** to make a sound, it moves backwards and forwards. Sometimes it is really easy to see a **vibration**:

Some vibrations are obvious – you can see where the sound is coming from

Road drill

Tuning fork

School bell

Elastic band

Guitar

But other times we can *hear* a sound without *seeing* a vibration. Even if we can't see a vibration, one must be happening if we hear a sound.

Some vibrations are invisible

CLARINET: When you blow, the sound comes from a vibrating column of air.

RADIO: When you switch it on the sound comes from the vibration of the loud**speaker cone.**

DRUM: When you hit it with a drumstick the sound comes from the vibration of the drum "skin".

Don't you believe me? You can see these 'invisible' vibrations with a little help:

- tap a drum with a drumstick;
- sprinkle some grains of rice or flour onto the drum skin; and
- watch what happens.

This works with loudspeakers too. You can see flour or talcum powder moving about on an old loudspeaker cone when it's switched on.
DON'T TRY THIS ON YOUR PARENTS' CD PLAYER!

Many of the sounds we hear every day come from radios, minidisc players or television sets. These work by making a **loudspeaker** vibrate.

Sound waves from a loud speaker

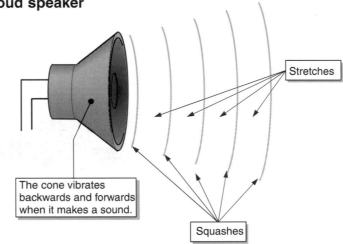

Stretches

The cone vibrates backwards and forwards when it makes a sound.

Squashes

How sounds reach our ears

When the cone of a loudspeaker is vibrating, it makes the air next to it vibrate as well. The air is 'squashed' and 'stretched' to make sound waves. These sound waves travel through the air until they reach our ears. When the vibrations reach our ears, they make our **eardrums** vibrate. These tiny pieces of skin can send a message to our brains and when this message reaches the brain we finally hear a sound.

This is how we hear a sound

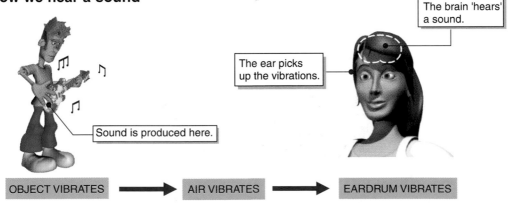

The brain 'hears' a sound.

The ear picks up the vibrations.

Sound is produced here.

OBJECT VIBRATES → AIR VIBRATES → EARDRUM VIBRATES

Sound needs a material to travel through

Sound waves must have something to pass through, or they can't travel from one place to another. Most of the sounds we hear travel through the air, but sound can also travel through other materials. These materials include liquids, such as water, and solids like brick, wood and glass.

Sounds are transmitted through solid, liquid or gas

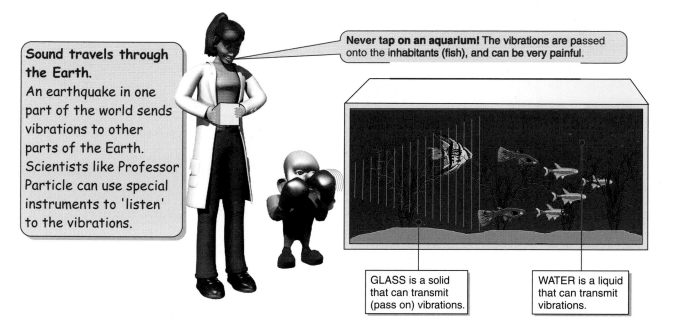

Sound travels through the Earth.

An earthquake in one part of the world sends vibrations to other parts of the Earth. Scientists like Professor Particle can use special instruments to 'listen' to the vibrations.

Never tap on an aquarium! The vibrations are passed onto the inhabitants (fish), and can be very painful.

GLASS is a solid that can transmit (pass on) vibrations.

WATER is a liquid that can transmit vibrations.

Sound waves are often changed when they pass through other materials. This is why sounds seem strange when we hear them underwater or through a wall. Some other animals have ears that are used to hearing sounds that seem very strange to us.

A Beluga or white whale. Whales and dolphins can 'talk' to each other by passing vibrations through the water. They can hear 'sounds' like these over hundreds of miles.

Sound cannot travel through a **vacuum**. A vacuum is an empty space, so there is no air, water or other material to be 'stretched' and 'squashed'.

Exercise 24.1: Sound

1. Complete this paragraph:

   Sounds are made when something .... Vibrations then travel through the .... to our ears. Vibrations can also travel through .... (such as water) and .... (such as brick). Animals such as .... are very good at hearing sounds under water.

2. Can sound travel through a vacuum? Explain your answer.

3. (a) Professor Particle plays a number of instruments to see which part of the instrument vibrates when a noise is made. Copy and fill in the blank spaces on her results chart (below).

Instrument	The part of the instrument that vibrates
Drum	
Clarinet	
Violin	
Guitar	
Xylophone	

   (b) Why does the guitar make a sound?

   (c) What would she see happening a few seconds after playing the guitar? What would she hear?

Extension question

4. Look at this diagram. Say what you would hear when the switch is closed. What would you hear when the pump is switched on? Give reasons for your answers.

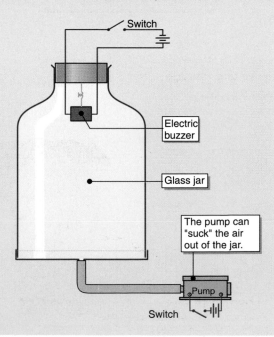

Switch

Electric buzzer

Glass jar

The pump can "suck" the air out of the jar.

Pump

Switch

Different sounds

It's important to remember that:

- sounds can only happen if an object vibrates; and
- we can only hear sounds if the vibration reaches our ears.

Not all sounds are the same. Some sounds are **louder** than others, and some sounds are **higher** ('squeakier') than others.

The loudness of sounds

As we now know, all sounds are caused by vibrations. Sometimes these vibrations are too small to see (see page 201), but sometimes they can be seen quite easily. If you start to play a guitar, you would be able to see the string vibrate as it makes a sound. You could make the sound *louder* if the string is plucked so hard that the vibrations are very large. The sound would be *quieter* (*softer*) if the string is plucked gently and the vibrations are quite small.

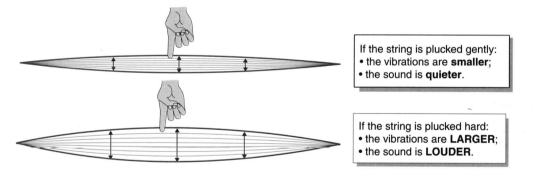

If the string is plucked gently:
• the vibrations are **smaller**;
• the sound is **quieter**.

If the string is plucked hard:
• the vibrations are **LARGER**;
• the sound is **LOUDER**.

Large vibrations in an object make bigger sound waves. A big sound wave has **more energy** than a small one and this is why it sounds louder. In other words, the harder you hit or pluck something the more energy there will be in a vibration from this object, and so the louder the sound will be.

Loudness depends on energy

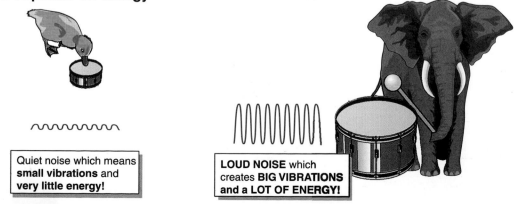

Quiet noise which means **small vibrations** and **very little energy!**

LOUD NOISE which creates **BIG VIBRATIONS** and a **LOT OF ENERGY!**

Pitch is another difference between sounds

The **pitch** of a sound is how high or low the sound is. There are several things that affect the pitch of a sound:

- the **size of the object** that is vibrating;
- the **mass of the object** that is vibrating.

Size alters the pitch of a sound

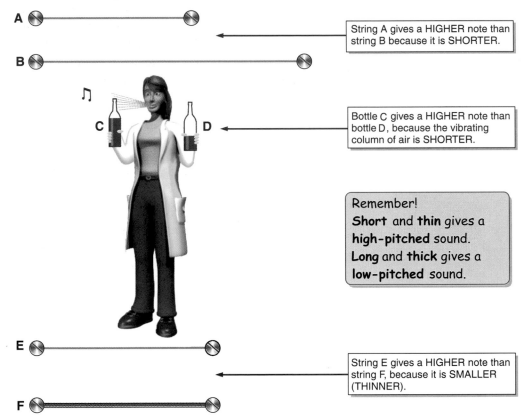

String A gives a HIGHER note than string B because it is SHORTER.

Bottle C gives a HIGHER note than bottle D, because the vibrating column of air is SHORTER.

Remember!
Short and **thin** gives a **high-pitched** sound.
Long and **thick** gives a **low-pitched** sound.

String E gives a HIGHER note than string F, because it is SMALLER (THINNER).

- The **tightness of the object** that is vibrating.

Tightness alters the pitch of a sound

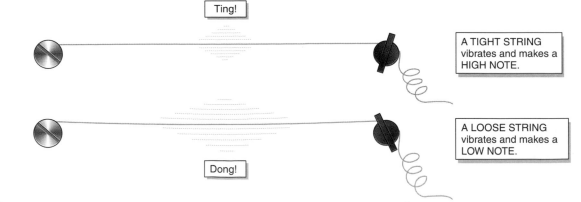

Ting!

A TIGHT STRING vibrates and makes a HIGH NOTE.

A LOOSE STRING vibrates and makes a LOW NOTE.

Dong!

The pitch of the sound depends on how many vibrations (how many 'squeezes' and 'stretches') are fitted into the same amount of time. Scientists can measure how many vibrations take place in a time as short as one second. If there are a lot of vibrations in one second, the sound will be very high ('squeaky') and if there are only a few vibrations in one second, the sound will be very low ('deep').

More vibrations give a higher pitch!

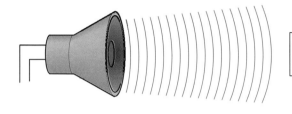

Many vibrations in a short time give out a HIGH-PITCHED sound.

Few vibrations in a short time give out a LOW-PITCHED sound.

You don't need to know this yet, but we will tell you anyway! The number of vibrations in one second is called the FREQUENCY of sound.

You can hear up to a frequency of about 18,000 vibrations per second.

Playing a stringed instrument

The sound you make from a stringed instrument depends on several different things, as shown in this diagram:

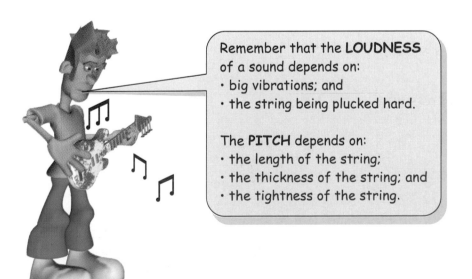

Remember that the **LOUDNESS** of a sound depends on:
• big vibrations; and
• the string being plucked hard.

The **PITCH** depends on:
• the length of the string;
• the thickness of the string; and
• the tightness of the string.

Exercise 24.2: Pitch and loudness

1. What is meant by the pitch of a sound?

2. Professor Particle's young nephew has two recorders, a long red one and a short blue one. Which has the higher pitch when he blows through them, the long one or the short one? Give a reason for your answer.

3. Keen to join the musical fun and games, Professor Particle gets out her old drum which has been gathering dust in the attic.

   (a) How would she make a quiet noise on the drum?

   (b) How would she make a loud noise?

   (c) How could she alter the drum, so that it made a lower-pitched sound?

   (d) What is meant by the term 'vibrate'?

4. She now tries to make a musical instrument. She has six empty bottles and some water. Suggest how she might make an instrument that could make a range of sounds from low to high. Say which bottle would make the highest pitched noise.

5. One of Professor Particle's students is not paying attention in the lab. Instead of listening to her, he is holding his ruler over the edge of the desk and flicking the end so that it vibrates.

   (a) The student's ruler is overhanging the desk by 30 cm. It makes a sound; why?

   (b) When he moves the ruler, so that 50 cm is overhanging the desk, what happens to the sound. Explain your answer.

   (c) How would he make a louder sound without changing the distance that the ruler was overhanging the desk?

   (d) What would he do to make a very loud, high-pitched sound?

Extension questions

6. Describe a fair test you could carry out to check if the length of a string affected the pitch of the sound made when the string is plucked.

7. Jack, another of Professor Particle's students, is very noisy! He wanted to check something about the loudness of sounds. He dropped different numbers of weights onto the floor, and used a sound-meter to find out the loudness of the sound. Here are the results of his experiment.

Number of weights	1	5	6	10	15	20	22
Loudness of sound (units on sound-meter)	3	14	18	29	43	59	65

   (a) Plot a graph of his results.

   (b) What is the pattern of his results?

   (c) Use the graph to work out the loudness of dropping 12 weights.

   (d) Give two things he had to do if this were to be a fair test.

   (e) Give one way in which he could have improved the experiment.

Chapter 25
The Earth and beyond

We live on the Earth, but we can see the Sun and the Moon quite clearly. We can see the Moon because it's quite close to us and reflects light from the Sun (see page 191) and we can see the Sun because it is very large and luminous.

The Sun is an enormous, very hot ball of glowing gas called a **star**. The Earth is much smaller and cooler, and is one of the **planets** that move around the Sun. The Sun, and the planets that move around it, make up our **solar system**.

The Sun and the Earth are part of our solar system

Remembering names can be quite difficult, so I find it helps to make up a silly story!

Photograph of my mum!

My
Very
Eccentric
Mother
Just
Shot
Uncle
Norman's
Pig

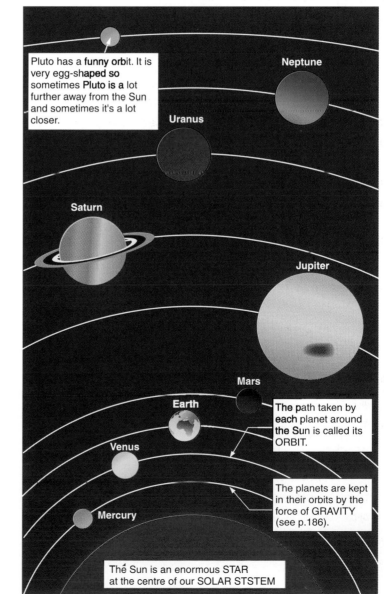

Pluto has a **funny orb**it. It is very egg-sha**ped so** sometimes **Pluto is a** lot further away from the Sun and sometimes it's a lot closer.

Neptune

Uranus

Saturn

Jupiter

Mars

Earth

Venus

Mercury

The path taken by **each** planet around **the S**un is called its ORBIT.

The planets are kept in their orbits by the force of GRAVITY (see p.186).

The Sun is an enormous STAR at the centre of our SOLAR STSTEM

When we look at the Sun, it looks round. It doesn't matter where we look from, or what time of the year it is, the Sun *always* looks round. This tells us that the Sun is a **sphere**. Astronauts travelling around the Earth have been able to take pictures that show us that the Earth and the Moon are also spheres.

Day and night

The way in which the Earth moves in space gives us day and night. The reasons for this are as follows:

- The Earth slowly spins around a line running from the North Pole to the South Pole. This line is called the **axis** of the Earth.
- It takes one **day** (24 hours) for the Earth to go through one complete turn.
- The Earth is always travelling around the Sun.
- The side of the Earth facing the Sun is lit up and so it's **daytime** on this side.
- The side of the Earth away from the Sun is in the dark and therefore it's **night-time** on this side.

Night and day

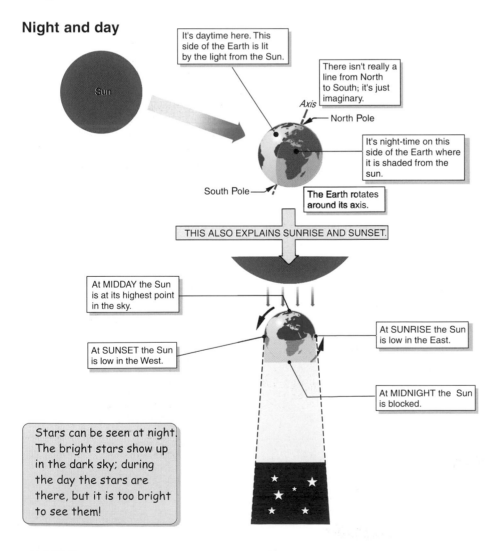

It's daytime here. This side of the Earth is lit by the light from the Sun.

There isn't really a line from North to South; it's just imaginary.

Axis

North Pole

Sun

It's night-time on this side of the Earth where it is shaded from the sun.

South Pole

The Earth rotates around its axis.

THIS ALSO EXPLAINS SUNRISE AND SUNSET.

At MIDDAY the Sun is at its highest point in the sky.

At SUNRISE the Sun is low in the East.

At SUNSET the Sun is low in the West.

At MIDNIGHT the Sun is blocked.

Stars can be seen at night. The bright stars show up in the dark sky; during the day the stars are there, but it is too bright to see them!

Sun and shadow

The Sun always stays in the same place which is at the centre of our solar system. The Sun *appears* to move across the sky as the day goes only because it is the Earth that is actually moving. Any object in the way of the Sun casts a **shadow** (see page 195). The size and direction of the shadow depends on where the Sun is when it shines on that object.

- Shadows are **short** at midday because the Sun is directly overhead.
- Shadows are **long** in the morning and the evening because the Sun is low in the sky.
- The shadows are always **on the opposite side** of the object from the Sun.

Sun and shadows

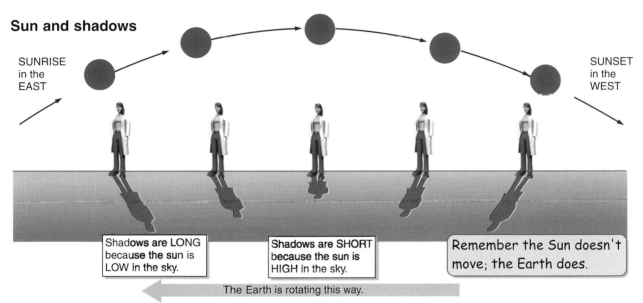

Sundials use these two rules to let us tell the time. We can make a scale that the shadow can fall on. As the shadow moves, it travels across the time scale and so tells us what time of day it is.

A sundial

Exercise 25.1: The Sun and the Earth

1. (a) Use a diagram to explain why it is midday in London at the same time that it's midnight in New Zealand.

   (b) Explain how day and night are caused.

2. Complete this paragraph:

   The Earth is a .... that moves around the .... The Sun is at the centre of the .... and is a very hot ball of glowing gas called a .... The .... travels around the Earth and we can see it because of light .... from the Sun.

3. (a) What shape is the Sun? How do we know?

   (b) How long does it take the Earth to make one orbit of the Sun?

   (c) What shape are the Earth and the Moon?

Extension questions

4. Why do stars only come out at night?

5. These two pictures of Professor Particle were taken at different times of the day: one at midday and one at six o'clock in the evening.

   (a) Which picture was taken at which time? Give a reason for your answer.

   (b) Which way was she facing (i.e. north, south, east or west) when the pictures were taken? Give a reason for your answer.

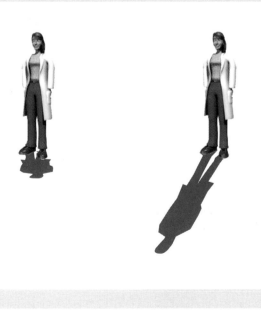

The year and the seasons

Remember

- The Sun is at the centre of the Solar System.
- The Earth is one of the planets that move around the Sun.
- The Earth rotates around a line called its axis.

What is a year?

The Earth moves around the Sun in an orbit. The Earth is kept in this orbit by the pull of the Sun's gravity. One **year** (actually 365 ¼ days) is the time taken for the Earth to complete one orbit.

The Earth rotates around its axis to give day and night (see page 210). The axis of the Earth isn't exactly upright. As you can see in the diagram below, it actually leans to one side, so that the North Pole and the South Pole don't get exactly the same amount of sunlight.

The tilting Earth – in June

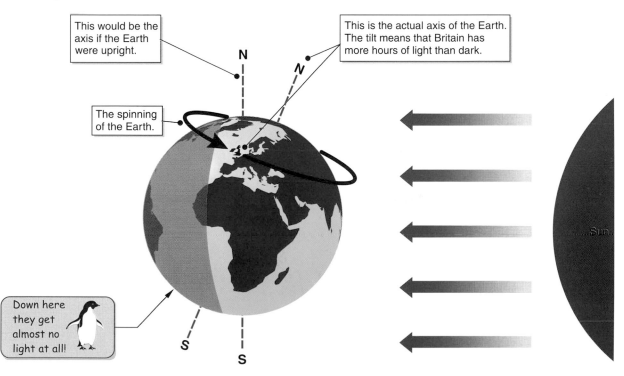

This would be the axis if the Earth were upright.

This is the actual axis of the Earth. The tilt means that Britain has more hours of light than dark.

The spinning of the Earth.

Down here they get almost no light at all!

Sun

During the course of a year the North Pole is sometimes nearest the Sun and sometimes furthest from the Sun. When the Earth is rotating with the North Pole *nearest* the Sun, it is summer in Britain and winter at the opposite end of the Earth, in Australia for example. It is winter in Britain when the Earth is rotating with the North Pole *away from* the Sun.

The tilt of the Earth gives us the **seasons**.

The tilting of the Earth gives us the seasons

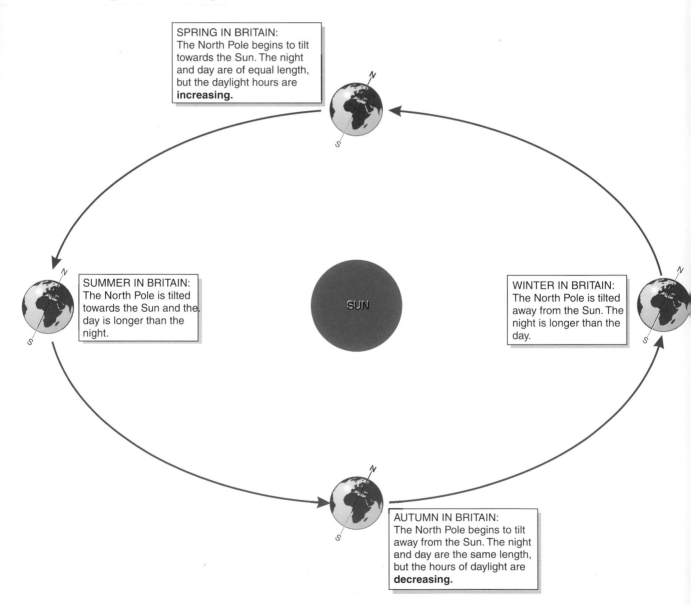

SPRING IN BRITAIN:
The North Pole begins to tilt towards the Sun. The night and day are of equal length, but the daylight hours are **increasing.**

SUMMER IN BRITAIN:
The North Pole is tilted towards the Sun and the day is longer than the night.

SUN

WINTER IN BRITAIN:
The North Pole is tilted away from the Sun. The night is longer than the day.

AUTUMN IN BRITAIN:
The North Pole begins to tilt away from the Sun. The night and day are the same length, but the hours of daylight are **decreasing.**

The height of the Sun varies from season to season

The Sun is highest in the sky at midday (12 noon) on any given day. The Sun appears in Britain to be at its greatest height in the sky, when the North Pole is tilted towards the Sun, i.e. in the summer.

Seasons affect the height of the Sun

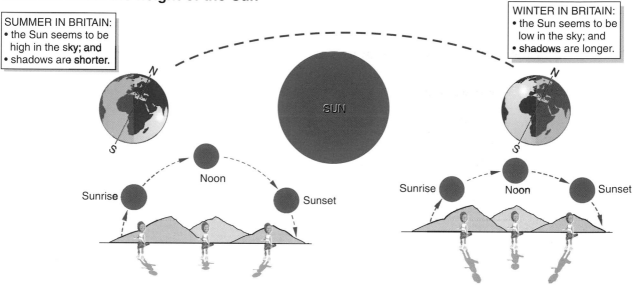

SUMMER IN BRITAIN:
• the Sun seems to be high in the sky; **and**
• shadows are **shorter.**

WINTER IN BRITAIN:
• the Sun seems to be low in the sky; **and**
• **shadows** are longer.

Remember that the height of the Sun affects the length of shadows (see page 211). The Sun is lowest during the winter, so the shadows on sunny days in winter are longer than those on sunny days in summer.

The Sun and the Earth

THE 365¼ DAY ORBIT of the Earth around the Sun gives us the YEAR.

THE 24-HOUR SPIN of the Earth gives us NIGHT and DAY.

THE TILT of the Earth gives us:
• the SEASONS; and
• the HEIGHT OF THE SUN IN THE SKY.

When the Sun is lower in the sky, it does not heat up the surface of the Earth as well as it does when it is high in the sky. Winter is colder because:

● the 'wintery' part of the Earth is further from the Sun; and

● the Sun is lower in the sky.

What about the Moon?

The Moon orbits the Earth. It takes about 28 days for the Moon to complete one orbit of the Earth. This length of time is called a **lunar month** (the word 'lunar' means 'to do with the Moon'). The Moon is kept in this orbit by the pull of the Earth's gravity.

The Moon does not give out its own light, but it does reflect light from the Sun. We see different amounts of reflected light at different times in the Moon's orbit around the Earth. The different views we get at different times of the month are called the **phases of the Moon**.

The Moon and its phases

Gravity on the Moon is less than on Earth, because the Moon is smaller. Astronauts can jump higher and longer on the Moon than on Earth.

The moon's orbit around the Earth takes 28 days.

The HALF MOON **gets** smaller every night. This is called a WANING MOON.

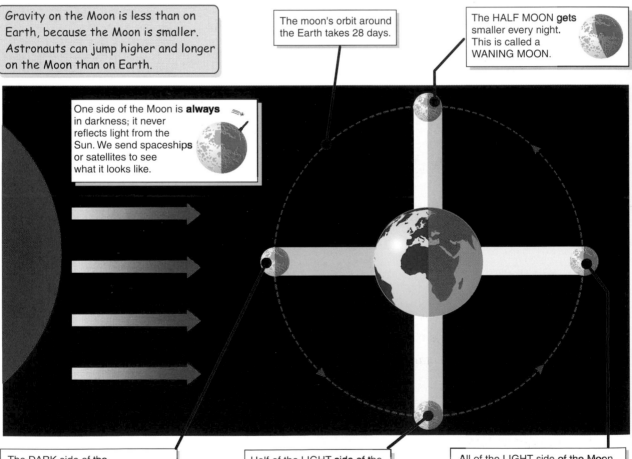

One side of the Moon is **always** in darkness; it never reflects light from the Sun. We send spaceships or satellites to see what it looks like.

The DARK side of **the** Moon is facing the **Earth**. We cannot see the **Moon** (except for a tiny **a**mount of light). This is called the NEW MOON.

Half of the LIGHT **side of the** Moon is facing th**e** Earth. We see the HALF MOON, getting bigger every night. This is called a WAXING MOON.

All of the LIGHT side **of the Moon** can be seen; it is facing the Earth and reflectin**g** the light of the Sun. This is called a FULL MOON.

Exercise 25.2: The Sun, the Earth and the Moon

1. How long does it take for:

   (a) The Earth to orbit the Sun?

   (b) The Moon to orbit the Earth?

   (c) The Earth to turn once on its axis?

2. (a) Name a man-made object that orbits the Earth.

   (b) Name one natural object that orbits the Earth.

3. Give two reasons why it is colder in winter than in summer.

4. Look at this diagram (not drawn to scale!).

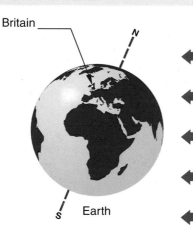

   (a) Copy it and shade in the part of the Earth that is in shadow.

   (b) Say whether it is summer or winter in Britain.

   (c) Say whether it is daytime or night-time in Britain.

5. Where on the Earth would you get almost no light at all during the British summer?

Extension questions

6. Find out what is meant by 'midnight sun'. Use a diagram to explain how it can happen.

7. How many times does the Moon orbit the Earth while the Earth completes one orbit of the Sun? Give a reason for your answer.

Expectations

At the end of this book

You should be able to:

- understand the processes of life, and see that humans are living things too;
- see that the properties of materials help to explain what they are used for;
- remember the most important physical processes that affect this planet and the other stars and planets in our Universe.

You may also be able to:

- design you own experiments to test out your theories about what you observe in the world around you.

At this stage we bid you farewell and look forward to seeing you again in Book 2!

Glossary

Section 1: Life and living processes

Adaptation   Acquiring some feature that makes an organism more suited to its environment.

Adolescence   A stage in the human life cycle where there is rapid physical and emotional development.

Adult   A human who has finished growing but can continue to learn.

Alcohol   A drug that affects many parts of the body, especially the nervous system.

Arteries   Blood vessels that carry blood away from the heart.

Backbone   Protects the spinal cord.

Balanced diet   An intake of food that provides all the correct nutrients in the right proportions.

Blood   A red fluid that can dissolve oxygen and foods.

Blood vessels   The arteries, capillaries and veins, that make sure that the blood circulates to the places it's needed.

Brain   An organ found in the head that controls many of the life processes in animals.

Canines   Killing teeth that are well-developed in carnivores.

Carbohydrates   A food substance including starches and sugars that supplies most of the energy we need.

Carpel   The female part of a flower – made up of stigma, style and ovary.

Childhood   The stage in the human life cycle just before adolescence – the child is still dependent on its parents for food and shelter.

Chlorophyll   A green pigment (colour) in plant cells that can absorb light energy for photosynthesis.

Collar bone   Helps to control arm movement.

Conservation   Caring for the environment for the benefit of living organisms.

Consumer   An organism in a food chain that eats other organisms.

Dietary fibre   The indigestible content of the food (largely from plant cell walls) which provide bulk for the faeces.

Dispersal   A process that spreads out seeds and fruits, so they can carry on their life processes without interference from the parent plants.

Embryo   An early stage in the development of a living organism before birth.

Endangered species   Living organisms that may not survive in the wild, usually due to human actions.

Fats   A food substance providing a supply of energy.

Fertilisation   The joining together of male and female sex cells.

Fertiliser   A mixture of minerals that can be added to the soil to help plants grow properly.

Fluoride   A mineral found in water which can help resist tooth decay.

Food chain   The passage of food energy between different living organisms – made up of producers and consumers.

Germination   The change from seed to a young plant.

Growth   A life process where an organism increases in size.

Habitat   A place where an organism lives – it must supply food, shelter and a breeding place.

Heart   An organ that pumps blood through all parts of an animal's body.

Hibernation   A way of avoiding harsh conditions by sleeping for a long period.

Incisors   Cutting teeth in the front of the jaw.

Insect   An invertebrate with three body parts, several pairs of legs and usually two pairs of wings.

Intestines   A long tube that runs from the mouth to the anus and breaks the food down, so that useful substances can be taken into the blood.

Invertebrate   An animal without a backbone.

Kidneys   Keep the body free of impurities, removing excess water from the blood, filtering out impurities made by the body and creating waste liquid called urine.

Leaf   Part of plant which traps sunlight.

Liver   An organ in the body dealing with food taken in by the intestines; it stores some useful parts of food and makes a lot of heat which helps keep the body warm.

Lungs   An organ that allows oxygen to enter the body.

Micro-organism (microbe)   A small organism that can only be seen with a microscope.

Migration   A way of avoiding harsh conditions by moving to a new habitat.

Milk teeth   The first set of baby teeth in humans.

Minerals   Substances that usually combine with another food to form different parts of the body, such as teeth, bones and red blood cells.

Molars   Grinding teeth at the side of the jaw.

Nicotine   Drug found in tobacco and responsible for causing addiction to smoking.

Nocturnal   Being active at night, like an owl.

Nutrition   The life process that provides a living organism with its food.

Obesity   An extremely heavy body weight that might cause illness.

Organ   One part of a body, with a special function – for example the heart which pumps blood around the body.

Organism   A living animal or plant.

Ovule   The part of the plant's ovary that contains the egg cell.

Pelvis   The link between the backbone and the legs.

Period   Periods or menstruation begin at the onset of puberty in girls.

Petal   Part of a flower, often brightly-coloured to attract insects for pollination.

Photosynthesis   Plant nutrition process that uses light energy to change carbon dioxide gas and water into food and oxygen.

Plaque   Sticky mixture of bacteria and sugar that can lead to tooth decay.

Pollination   The transfer of the male sex cell, or pollen grain, from the anther to the stigma of a flower.

Predator   An animal that hunts and captures other animals.

Pre-molars   Teeth-like scissors in carnivores, to tear and grind food.

Prey   An animal hunted and captured by other animals.

Producer   A green plant in a food chain that can produce food for other organisms.

Protein   A food substance used in the growth and repair of cells.

Puberty   Changes during adolescence leading to sexual maturity.

Pubic hair   The hair that grows around the genitals at the onset of puberty.

Pulse   The stretching of artery walls caused by the beating of the heart.

Reproduction   The life process that produces new individual organisms.

Ribcage   Protects the heart and lungs.

Roots   Absorb water and minerals from the soils; they also anchor the plant firmly in the soil.

Seed   What develops if an ovule is fertilised.

Sepal   The outer layer of a flower which protects the other flower parts.

Shoulder blade   Bone which stops your arm going too far backwards.

Spider   An invertebrate with two body parts and eight legs.

Stamen   The male part of a flower.

Stamina   The ability to keep working or exercising for a long time.

Stem   Part of the plant supporting the leaves holding them up towards the light.

Stomach   A part of the body which stores food, and churns and mixes it up with chemicals helping to break it down.

Veins   Blood vessels that bring blood back to the heart.

Vitamins   Substances needed in very small amounts to enable the body to use other nutrients more efficiently.

Vertebrate   An animal with a backbone (as part of a bony skeleton).

Materials and their properties

Alloy   A combination of metals and other substances which is stronger or better in some way than the component parts.

Basalt   Rock formed from magma that has cooled down.

Boiling   A physical change in which heat changes a liquid into a gas (for example, liquid water into water vapour).

Chemical change   A reaction that makes new substances and cannot be reversed.

Concrete   A man-made building material produced from mixing together several natural materials.

Condensation   A physical change in which cooling a gas changes it into a liquid.

Conductor   A material that allows something to pass through it (for example, a metal wire is a conductor because it allows electricity to pass through it).

Convection   The passage of heat through liquids or gasses by means of currents.

Corrosion   A change to a metal caused by reaction with something in the air.

Decanting   A way of separating a solid from a liquid by letting the solid settle and then pouring the liquid into another container.

Dissolving   A process that spreads out particles of a solid through a liquid to produce a solution.

Evaporation   A physical process in which a liquid changes into a gas. This process requires heat.

Filtrate   The liquid that passes through a filter.

Filtration   A process that uses a filter (like a sieve) to separate a solid from a liquid.

Fossil fuel   A fuel that was made millions of years ago from the bodies of dead animals and plants.

Freezing   The change of a liquid to a solid as the temperature falls (e.g., liquid water changing to ice).

Fuel   A material that can be used to release energy.

Gas   A substance with particles so far apart that it occupies an enormous space and can easily change its shape.

Granite   Rock formed from magma that has cooled down and hardened inside the Earth's crust.

Humus   Sticky material in soil made by the decay of dead animals and plants.

Insoluble   Will not dissolve in a liquid (for example, sand is insoluble in water).

Insulator   A material that will not allow something to pass through (for example, polystyrene is an insulator because it will not let heat pass through it).

Liquid   A substance with particles that are only attached loosely to one another so that the substance can easily flow from one place to another.

Loam   An ideal soil for growing plants. It has the correct mixture of rock particles, air, water, minerals and humus.

Magma   Liquid rock found inside the Earth.

Magnet   A substance that can attract a metal such as iron.

Melting   A physical process in which heat changes a solid to a liquid (for example, ice can melt into liquid water).

Metal   A material that is hard, can be polished and usually conducts heat and electricity.

Mixture   A collection made up of several different materials that can be separated by a reversible physical process.

Opaque   Light cannot pass through an opaque material.

Permeability   Allows a liquid to pass through (for example, a soil with high permeability lets water pass through very easily).

Physical change   A process in which no new materials are made and which can be reversed.

Radiation   The passage of heat from the Sun.

Residue   The material left on a filter when a mixture is poured through it.

Reversible   Can be changed back to what it was (for example, the change between ice and water is reversible).

Rusting   A process in which air and water cause a chemical change to iron.

Sieving   Using a mesh to separate a mixture of solid particles of different sizes.

Solid   A substance with its particles so close together that it is very difficult to alter its shape.

Soluble   Able to dissolve in a liquid (for example, salt is soluble in water).

Solute   A substance that can dissolve in a liquid (called the solvent) to form a solution.

Solution   What is formed when a solute dissolves in a solvent.

Solvent   The liquid that can dissolve a solute to form a solution.

Temperature   A measure of hotness or coldness.

Texture   The 'feel' of a substance (for example, some rocks have a very rough texture).

Thermal   Means 'to do with heat'.

Thermometer   An instrument for measuring temperature.

Tooth decay   Caused by bacteria changing sugar into acid which then eats away at the hard enamel covering the teeth, making a hole which finally reaches the soft insides.

Transparent   We can see through a transparent material. Light can pass through without changing the light rays, so the image is clear.

Wisdom teeth   Four molars that may appear in late teens or early twenties.

Water cycle   The change of water between solid, liquid and gas that circulates water around the planet Earth.

Physical Processes

Air resistance   Friction between an object and the air.

Appliance   Something in the home that uses power (for example, a TV is an appliance).

Attract   To pull together (for example, opposite poles of a magnet attract each other).

Balanced forces   Two forces of the same size that are pushing in opposite directions.

Battery   A source of power in a circuit (a battery can have several cells in it).

Cell   A source of power in which chemical reactions produce electrical charge.

Charge   A small amount of electricity.

Circuit   A source of power and some electrical components arranged together, so that electric current can flow.

Compass   An instrument which shows the direction of the Earth's magnetic field and is for navigation.

Component   One of the pieces that makes up an electrical circuit (for example, a bulb is a component).

Conductor   A material allowing electrical current to pass through it.

Current   The flow of charge around a circuit.

Day   The time taken for the Earth to spin once around its axis.

Eardrum   The part of the ear that vibrates when a sound reaches it.

Expansion   Getting bigger.

Force   Something causing a change in the speed or the direction of movement.

Friction   A force between two objects when they rub together.

Gravity   The force that pulls objects together (for example, gravity is the force that pulls us towards the centre of the Earth).

Image   What we see when we look at an object.

Insulator   A material that does not allow electrical current to pass through it.

Loudness   A measure of the intensity of a sound – in other words, how much energy the sound has.

Luminous   Giving out light (for example, the Sun is a luminous object).

Month   The length of time taken for the Moon to orbit the Earth.

Motor   A component that changes electrical energy into movement.

Newton   A unit of force.

Opaque   Does not allow light to pass through it.

Orbit   The path of one object around another.

Pitch   How high or low a sound is.

Poles   The two ends of a magnet.

Ray   The pathway that light travels.

Ray diagram   A drawing showing how light travels.

Reflecting   Bouncing back from an object; for example, the Moon is a reflecting body that bounces light back from the Sun to the Earth.

Repel   To push away (for example, the same poles of a magnet repel one another).

Series   A circuit with all of the components connected one after another – there is no choice for the pathway of the current.

Shadow   An area behind an opaque object opposite to a light source.

Short circuit   An easy route between the terminals of a power source in a circuit.

Sound wave   The way sound energy travels from place to place.

Switch   A component controlling the flow of electricity through a circuit.

Translucent   Allows light to pass through but changes the light rays, so that the image is unclear.

Transparent   Allows light to pass through without changing the light rays, so that the image is clear.

Vacuum   A space with no particles in it.

Vibration   A movement of an object – there is no sound without vibration.

Year   The length of time taken for the Earth to complete one orbit of the Sun.

Index